To our parents,
with love and gratitude

PRAISE FOR *THE ART OF CONDOLENCE* . . .

"*The Art of Condolence* is compassionate, thorough, and above all, practical."—*MINNEAPOLIS STAR TRIBUNE*

"Relying on an impressive variety of life experiences, the Zunins share their expertise throughout each and every page of this helpful book. *The Art of Condolence* effectively blends insightful knowledge of the grief process with practical ways of expressing one's care and concern for others."
—*CAREGIVERS QUARTERLY*

"While there are very few answers to the cosmic questions about who lives and who dies in what has become the Age of Grief for many gay men and lesbians, for those who want to comfort and condole but don't know what to say or do, Leonard and Hilary Zunin have come up with some timely answers."—*THE ADVOCATE*

"A useful volume to help folks through what is always an awkward and difficult time."—*PHILADELPHIA INQUIRER*

The Art of Condolence

What to Write, What to Say, What to Do at a Time of Loss

Leonard M. Zunin, M.D., and Hilary Stanton Zunin

HarperPerennial
A Division of HarperCollins*Publishers*

Copyright acknowledgments follow index.

A hardcover edition of this book was published in 1991 by HarperCollins Publishers.

HarperCollins books may be purchased for educational, business, or sales promotional use. For information, please call or write: Special Markets Department, HarperCollins Publishers, Inc., 10 East 53rd Street, New York, NY 10022. Telephone: (212) 207-7528; Fax: (212) 207-7222.

First HarperPerennial edition published 1992.

Designed by Irving Perkins Associates

The Library of Congress has catalogued the hardcover edition as follows:

Zunin, Leonard, 1936–
The art of condolence : what to write, what to say, what to do at a time of loss / Leonard M. Zunin, M.D., and Hilary Stanton Zunin.—1st ed.
p. cm.
Includes index.
ISBN 0-06-016437-9
1. Consolation. I. Zunin, Hilary Stanton, 1951– . II. Title.
BV4905.2.Z87 1991
306.9—dc20 90–55945

ISBN 0-06-092166-8 (pbk.)
92 93 94 95 96 AC/MB 10 9 8 7 6 5 4 3 2 1

Contents

Acknowledgments

Nearly four years ago we accepted the challenge of this project together, and together we wish to express our gratitude to all those who helped *The Art of Condolence* come to be.

We are deeply grateful to those friends, relatives, and professional associates who contributed their invaluable suggestions, insights, and support: Marina Aritheri, M.D., Lynn Bains, M.A., Edwin P. Brennan, M.D., Nancy S. Brennan, Eric Butler, Barbara Fetesoff, M.L.S., Jason A. Gross, Steven R. Johnson, Jeru Kabbal, Susan Kane, Monica Lehner-Kahn, Joyce Manning, Jessica Merrill, Diane Meyers, R.N., M.S.N., Lou and Judy Niemerow, Charman Palmer, M.D., Sydney Salmon, M.D., Jennifer A. Scarano, Ina H. Scarano, R.N., Ph.D., Victor R. Scarano, M.D., JD.L., Brenda Soobis, Ed and Mary Ann Stanton, Sydney Stanton, Tom Stanton, Cynthia Ruth Tarango, Helaina Zunin Taylor, Don and Marie Woolf, Ira David Zunin, and Louis and Betty Zunin. Special thanks to Norm Badion, Head of Reference, and the staff of the Napa City/County Library.

A particular note of appreciation to our European colleagues. Their sensitivity is a blessing to all with whom they work, and their attitude toward life's end is an inspiration: Yves Camberlein, M.D., Director, Unité de Soins Palliatifs, Hôpital International de l'Université de Paris; Brigitte Champenois, M.D., Director, Unité Mobile de Medicine Palliative, and her associate, Didier Coupez, M.D., Chief of Service, O.R.L., de l'Hôpital Saint-Joseph, Paris; and W. F. Vork, Director, Uitvaartcentrum Zuid, Amsterdam.

Throughout our research and work in this field we have been especially influenced and moved by the pioneering efforts of J. Bowlby, M.D., Rabbi Earl A. Grollman, Elisabeth Kübler-Ross, M.D., Stephen Levine, Colin Murray Parkes, M.D., Beverly Raphael, M.D., Dame Cicely Saunders, M.D., and J. William Worden, Ph.D.

Particular acknowledgment is due to Judith Riven for her vision and support. Sincere thanks are also due to Barbara Lowenstein, our agent, who from the outset had faith in the project, provided excellent input, and actively and enthusiastically represented the work. Heartfelt appreciation to our editor at HarperCollins, Janet Goldstein, for her sensitive understanding of the material and perceptive suggestions. We also appreciated the commitment to excellence of her assistant, Peternelle van Arsdale.

This work grew, in large part, out of our individual spiritual journeys. Spirituality often flowers in the sacred ground of loss. It is, therefore, with a thankfulness beyond thanks that we acknowledge the profound influence of the following contemporary spiritual leaders: Lama Thubten Yeshe, Lama Zopa Rinpoche, Osho, Ram Dass, Alan Watts, J. Krishnamurti, Da Free John, and Emmanuel.

So many people, including the widows of Operation Second Life, skydiving friends, patients, and students have shared with us their intimate experiences of grief and condolence. They have contributed letters of condolence, both written and received, and have brought to our attention anecdotes and quotes they found helpful and healing in times of loss. All have let us into their hearts and their sorrow and have helped illuminate the path that leads to healing.

Preface

This is a book about a shared human concern, a shared challenge, and a shared hope—how to sensitively reach out to another at a time of loss. While grief is indeed a normal process, and many people fully recover with little help, the vast majority of individuals who are mourning the death of a loved one benefit immensely from the condoling words and actions of those around them.

Often, those who sincerely wish to condole find their desire to help tightly bound by a sense of helplessness. As much as we care for a grieving friend or family member, we cannot bring back the dead and we cannot take the bereaved's grief away. There simply are no stock phrases or pat answers. On the contrary, when confronted by the anguish of another's grief, words seem to slip through our fingers like sand. But this book is about what we *can* do, not what we can't. Knowing what to write, say, and do is much simpler than one might think. In workshops, lectures, and private consultations we have assisted numerous individuals to find a new confidence in their ability to help those who mourn by following the simple suggestions and guidelines offered in this book.

One of us is a psychiatrist who, for more than twenty years, has been concerned with issues facing the bereaved and the terminally ill. The other is a teacher of English whose special interests have been the theme of loss and life's transitions as expressed in literature and the effect of grief on school-aged children.

In 1967, while serving as assistant chief, and later as chief, of neuropsychiatry at Camp Pendleton, California, I (Leonard M. Zunin) treated psychiatric casualties returning from Vietnam. But my attention and heart were also drawn to another troubled group on the base who were not actively seeking help. These were the recent widows of the men who hadn't returned at all.

Consulting with the late eminent psychiatrist Dr. Fritz Perls, I presented my vision of a special program for these bereaved women. Dr. Perls listened intently. Then, quietly and provocatively, he said, "This is a group of women you will have to teach how to say good-bye."

The resulting project, Operation Second Life, received national media attention and was responsible for assisting hundreds of widows to move through their grief and into a new life. In group session after session, the women not only taught each other about living through loss, they also taught me.

In helping these widows readjust to a life without their husbands, I grew to appreciate the power, depth, and transforming potential of the grief experience. I also was struck by the immense difficulty faced by most of the widows' friends and loved ones as they struggled to condole. Thus began my lifelong interest in attachment and loss, and the ways we all say hello and good-bye.

Later, my private psychiatric practice included many patients who were terminally ill. These courageous people had entered psychotherapy in the face of their imminent death in order to confront issues of quality and authenticity in the rest of their life. They, too, taught me much.

Challenged and inspired by my patients and their questions, my attention turned to aspects of personal transformation that led to a period of intense spiritual study and brought me to Nepal, India, and the Far East.

Another dimension was added to my work with loss when, following the San Francisco earthquake of 1989, I did grief support work with victims of the disaster and also conducted "debriefing" groups to assist caregivers who had provided service to the victims.

* * *

On a balmy spring day in 1973, I (Hilary Stanton Zunin) was a parachute rigger and jumpmaster skydiving at an airstrip surrounded by lush farmland outside of Madison,

Wisconsin. It was my last day in the area before moving cross country to take a full-time job at a sport skydiving center near San Francisco. The day was full of good-byes. The drop zone was animated by the slap of multicolored parachutes opening against a deep blue sky and the endless droning of the engine as the Cessna sailed up and down the runway. When a young friend and new skydiver, Jim Martin, asked if I would watch him from the ground as he made his seventh jump, I laughingly agreed. He was trying out a new set of gear he hoped to buy and couldn't wait to see it open over his head. Jim's dad, a career army man, wasn't on the drop zone that day, but his mom was.

That afternoon the winds were coming from the southwest, unusual for the area. Typically they blew in from due west. Maybe that was the problem. The ground must have seemed unfamiliar from Jimmy's vantage point. Or maybe it was his preoccupation once the new orange and white parachute opened above his head. No one would ever know for sure. All we could see from the runway was Jimmy headed for high-tension electric towers and a flash of blue fire as his parachute struck.

In the terror of the moment I grabbed Jim's mother's hand. The rest of the skydivers, all men, either ran toward the scene or walked uncomfortably away from us. Both of us denied what we'd seen. I assured Mrs. Martin that Jim *must* be all right. He was a heads-up kid, the best student we'd ever seen. It must have been his parachute that flamed so brightly. It must have been.

In the next hour, and for the next lifetime, we waited in a corner of the ramshackle building that was the skydiving club's base of operations. I don't recall my thoughts, but I remember that I held her as we rocked together in silence. When one of the guys finally called me out of the hut it was to ask, "Does she know?"

A shiver ran through my body and I whispered, "Know what?"

"Well, he's dead, of course. You'll have to tell her."

I suppose I was in shock. I know that when I reentered the shadowy room I had no idea what I was going to say. Mrs. Martin looked very small in the corner; she was about thirty-five years old and Jim was her only child. I didn't have to say anything. When she looked at me she knew.

"Oh, God! He's dead, isn't he? He's dead," she cried over and over. "Hilary, he's dead."

When I nodded, there was nothing left to say. We held one another and wept until her husband came. After I left them I walked the length of the runway to a deep green field, stumbled into the center, dropped to my knees, and started to breathe again.

As I turned my eyes upward I remember seeing one small white cloud. That was Jimmy, I thought. Something had changed in my life. Something was lost and something was found. I had never felt so much pain. But mixed with the pain was a confusing yet clear and overwhelming sense that, in that moment, I was connected with everything, even that small white cloud.

The Art of Condolence, gleaned from the experience of hundreds of bereaved and condolers alike, is both informative and inspiring reading. We hope that it will draw you to continue to explore the heart and the art of helping others at a time of loss. This practical resource operates on two levels. A complete reading will impart a broad understanding of issues surrounding condolence that can be invaluable no matter what the specific situation of loss. However, the book is also designed as a quick reference guide so you can easily turn to a particular area of need or topic of interest.

We strongly believe that all of us, whether trained professionals or the lay public, can serve ourselves and others by learning how to help the bereaved to say good-bye. This book will assist you to reach out more readily, more comfortably, and more authentically when confronted by another's grief.

Except where permission has been obtained, all names and all identifying characteristics of individuals mentioned have been altered in order to protect their privacy.

Part I

The Healing Journey

Can I see another's woe
And not be in sorrow too?
Can I see another's grief,
And not seek for kind relief?

—William Blake

Chapter 1

Why Condole?

Condole: To express sympathy or sorrow; I condoled with him in his loss.

—American Heritage Dictionary

I'M SO SORRY

You read it in the newspaper or the telephone rings; the loved one of a friend has died. Among the thoughts that cross your mind are the desire to help in some way, to respond to your friend's sorrow and pain. The wish to condole is such a human trait, yet most of us are at a loss to acknowledge, in a caring and loving way, the grief of others. That's understandable. No one has ever taught us the art of condolence. And when we try to draw from our own experiences of loss, we find that those who have tried to condole us, friends and relations with the best of intentions, have frequently said or done exactly the wrong thing.

We want to comfort, to condole, but we don't know what to write, what to say, or what to do. Days fade into each other and the call never seems to be made; that letter just never seems to get written. Sound familiar?

What is it about our confrontation with another's anguish that causes a tightness in our chest, a constriction in our throat, the primal urge, tempered only by social form, to run? What causes the words to slip away when we are faced with another's grief? Is it overwhelming compassion, or is it the reflection of our own mortality mirrored in another's suffering? Sometimes, when we respond to the grief of others, our deepest fears surface and we are reminded of our own experiences with the pain of loss. Yet, we know intuitively that in offering comfort and sympathy to another, each of us gains.

Grieving embraces the mysterious, unknowable aspects of existence and has the possibility of lending insight into oneself, one's choices, and the profound human longing to understand. Those who grieve, as well as those who have died, can become catalysts to stimulate our perceptions, help us reassess our priorities, and enhance our lives. Just as we grow by accepting solace from others, when we offer comfort and understanding we also grow.

The rewards are intrinsic: We feel good; we feel human; we feel real. And it doesn't happen all the time, but there are moments when such service yields an experience that goes far beyond simply feeling good. In their inspiring book, *How Can I Help?*, Ram Dass and Paul Gorman recognize these times, "in service itself—comforting a crying child, reassuring a frightened patient, bringing a glass of water to a bedridden elder—when you feel yourself to be a vehicle of kindness, an instrument of love. There's more to the deed than the doer and what's been done. You yourself feel transformed and connected to a deeper sense of identity" (p. 39).

The origin of the word *condolence* holds a profound message. There are two Latin roots: *com,* meaning "together," and *dolere,* meaning "to grieve." Condoling actions reaffirm our bonds to humanity; they strengthen and enlarge each of us. Each word of comfort, each letter of condolence, each act of helpful service has the potential to serve not only as a message of sympathy but as a song of compassion and truth.

HELPING THOSE WHO GRIEVE

At a workshop on loss, Gretchen, a well-spoken and successful executive, poignantly shared her surprising feelings of inadequacy when confronted with a situation that called for her to respond to someone in grief. While in a business meeting, she received an urgent phone call. It was a good friend who had just heard terrible news. The friend's mother had been killed in a car accident. Gretchen related, "She was choking on her words, gasping and asking me to come to her office and drive her home." Though the accident had happened several months before, Gretchen vividly recalled her profound anxiety. "I wanted to be sympathetic; after all, this was a close friend in pain. But the feeling that dominated wasn't sympathy; it was helplessness. I, who always had the right answers, was on the edge of panic. What could I do? How could I help?"

Like Gretchen, most people confronted with similar situations reel with unspoken questions and self-doubt: I have no idea what to do. What can I possibly say? Should I talk? What if I say the wrong thing? Should I go to them? Should I leave them alone? How can I best respond?

Over the years, we have explored numerous ways to provide comfort to others in times of loss. There is much to be learned from those who have experienced grief and those who have studied loss and the approaches that lend help, dignity, and support to the bereaved. Of course, as with every art, there are aspects of condolence that cannot be taught, but a clear understanding of specific helping ways has the potential to enhance both your own confidence and the comfort you provide.

It's crucial to recognize that while condoling actions can ease the pain and provide support, they will not stop the bereaved's feeling of loss. It wouldn't be good if they did. Grief is a healing process that should be allowed to run its course. There are no quick fixes or easy answers. There are, however, many things you can do to help those in grief.

TO ERR IS HUMAN . . . VERY HUMAN

Above all else, don't withdraw from responding to another's loss for fear of writing, saying, or doing the "wrong thing."

There will be times when you make a mistake or upon reflection you feel you could have said or done something better or more sensitively. Everybody makes mistakes. At the funeral of a wonderful ninety-year-old man we were standing with Bill, his bereaved son. Another friend approached to express his condolences. "I was so sorry to hear about your dad. What a remarkable man he was." Reaching out and placing his hand gently on Bill's shoulder, he went on. "You must feel very blessed to have had him in your life so long."

Bill's response was immediate and explosive. He slapped away his friend's hand and cried out, "Who the hell do you think you are to tell me I am blessed by my father's death. I don't care how old he was. I loved him and his death is no blessing!" In the awkward moment that followed the condoling friend blanched. It might have been easier for him to walk away, but fumbling for words, he went on, "My God, you're right. What a foolish thing to have said. Thank you, I really am very sorry."

Embracing his friend, Bill began to cry. "I'm sorry, too, and I'm glad you're here." A door had opened for these two men. A door opened by the extended hand of condolence and the willingness to put an innocent mistake aside.

Be gentle with yourself. Don't ask for perfection. That you are reading this book is a strong indication that you are open to learning and available to that part of you that so humanely cares to comfort others in times of loss. But one of the essential elements in condolence is accepting the bereaved as they are. Keep this in mind for yourself as well.

As you read various chapters in this book you may recognize "mistakes" you have made in the past. If this occurs, do two things. First, take a moment to appreciate your awareness and willingness to acknowledge the error. Second, learn from the incident. If, when trying to condole, you say or do something "inappropriate," make simple amends and then drop it. When you condemn yourself and feel guilty for the mistake, you focus on the guilt and not the lesson. The mistake is yours, but so is the gift of learning from it. In Chapter 4, in the section Words of Caution, we point out a few of the more common pitfalls.

THE LESSONS OF CONDOLENCE

Beyond the obvious and invaluable assistance that your healing actions provide to those touched by grief, the learning for yourself that comes from this heartfelt service is threefold. First, it teaches more about the power, mystery, and value of relationships. Second, it is a forceful reminder of the preciousness of life, and it compels you to examine your priorities. Third, condoling actions help you to build a stronger network of coping strategies in order to face more effectively the losses that are always around the corner in everyone's life.

Of course, there is no reason why we cannot bring this caring quality to any human interaction. The opportunity to draw on our generosity of heart and unity of spirit is always present when we are with others in need. Bereavement and condolence are among the deepest invitations and initiations into the enigma of human life—invitations that are in many ways more profound than joy or love. They provide a powerful challenge to our trust in the mystery of existence. When we meet that challenge, we meet our true selves.

What happens when your sincere condoling actions seem to go unappreciated? So often we have spoken with people who have reached out in compassion only to feel that they and their efforts were not appropriately acknowledged. This lack of a positive response from those in grief is frequently misunderstood. We think they don't value our help and, as a result, we sometimes pull away. But in the course of caring interactions, the benefit of someone's helping is often not appreciated in the moment it occurs.

If you expect gratitude for your condoling efforts, then reevaluate your motives. First, those in deep emotional pain are typically preoccupied, if not obsessed, with their own problems. The focus of the bereaved is on their lost loved one, not on you, and this yearning for the absent person engulfs them. The newly bereaved have little room for gratitude. Often, however, you'll find an unexpected sense of gratitude rising within you, the condoler. When another's suffering opens a new door into your heart, how can you not feel gratitude for the experience of being put in touch with a deeper part of yourself?

Chapter 2

The Phases of Grief

This book is about condolence, about the many ways each of us can reach out to help another at a time of loss. It is not a book about grief. Yet, by taking time to understand something of the healing journey that is grief and its natural progression, we as condolers become better equipped to respond to the bereaved. Researcher Bill Bridges, in his book *Transitions: Making Sense of Life's Changes,* notes that "to make a successful new beginning requires more than simply persevering. It requires an understanding of external signs and inner signals that point the way to the future."

As challenging, difficult, and tragic as it is, the loss of a loved one is not rare. In the United States, more than eight million people mourn the death of a close family member each year. Loss is an intimate and integral part of life, so the process of grieving is also an inescapable part of life.

Many excellent books deal exclusively with grief, and we've included suggested readings on this topic at the end of the book. Chapter 18 contains a discussion of abnormal grief, sometimes called "pathological grief."

This chapter presents an overview of what, for most people, is a *normal grief response.* The reactions described most closely fit the kind of grief that follows the loss of a very close loved one, such as a spouse. Most other losses will provoke similar responses but with varying degrees of intensity.

Beginning in denial and ending in resolution, grief's path winds through confusing and often unfamiliar terrain. Nevertheless, while subject to cultural and religious influences, certain basic characteristics of the grieving process are common to everyone. For the purposes of this discussion we have divided grief into three phases: (1) shock, numbness, and disbelief; (2) experiencing the pain; and (3) resolution and acceptance. As Larry Cochran and Emily Claspell explain in *The Meaning of Grief:*

> People who grieve tend to review the situation of loss, seeking information that would help them understand what they are experiencing. Some read literature on grief. Some recall past experiences of loss. Others talk to or try to learn from someone else who has experienced a loss. By finding out more about grief or loss, people hope to put the experience in a meaningful perspective, become familiar with what to expect, and mobilize their resources.

Saying good-bye takes time. Having some understanding of grief often helps the bereaved in the coping and healing process. Knowing what to expect during mourning can diminish anxiety, be useful in preparing for the challenges ahead, and provide an understanding that fosters hope. In addition, the urge to know more about grief is a healthy aspect of the process itself. It represents the realistic expectation that in time the pain of loss will be transformed into a new way of being.

LET THE HEALING BEGIN

The profound experience of grief is neither a disease nor a disorder. It has more in common with the body's response to an injury. We're used to thinking of grief as an overwhelming burden of anguish and sadness. Of course, there is great pain, but in a larger sense, grief is the way the psyche heals itself. When you break an arm or a leg there is an organized and predictable series of cellular reactions that you recognize as healing. This is also true at a psychological level; the loss of a loved one is experienced as a wound to the fabric of our being. Loss also initiates a healing process. It is this process that enables those of us who have lost a loved one to live anew and to reestablish the balance and continuity of our life.

Grief is a time when every aspect of the relationship with a loved one is felt, examined, and reexamined including experiences, hopes, feelings, thoughts, and memories. While in one sense bereavement lasts for a number of months or years, in another sense it initiates a transformation that has no end. At unexpected moments, ripples of remembrance and sorrow will surface for the rest of our life. It may not seem like it, and it certainly doesn't feel like it, but the pain of grieving is as much an integral part of our natural life experience as the pleasure and joy of loving. The risk of love is loss, and the price of loss is grief.

There is unending variation in the way people respond to bereavement. These responses cannot be plotted in a series of neatly defined steps, nor is the progression from the time of loss to the resolution of bereavement likely to travel in a straight line. Rather, grief involves a succession of responses that fade into and replace one another. Though confusing in many ways, bereavement has its own internal logic. Even its most painful aspects serve a purpose. Each path of grief will take a unique course, yet there are certain signposts of bereavement common to all those who pass along this road. Grief is not a static state of being; it is a journey, an ever-changing process.

Shock, Numbness, and Disbelief

It doesn't seem to matter whether the loss was anticipated or not; the first response is *profound shock.* The bereaved may cry out, feeling as if they've received a physical blow. Just as the body goes into shock after a serious injury, the mind and spirit go into shock when confronted with a severe emotional jolt. This sensation is rapidly followed by *disbelief* and *numbness.* Emily Dickinson called it the "hour of lead."

For the bereaved, it just doesn't seem possible that a person who has meant so much will no longer be part of their life, so the first and natural reaction is to doubt or deny the death itself. Sometimes, for brief periods, this effort even succeeds. Those in grief frequently find themselves saying, "There must be some mistake," or "It's just not true." This denial phase is critical; it's an unconscious way of preventing emotional overload. It helps the bereaved face the loss bit by bit as they gather their inner resources and outer supports.

A sensation of numbness often occurs at the same time. Again, this is an unconsciously intelligent response. It doesn't mean that those in grief are cold or unfeeling; rather, it is nature's way of sheltering them as it exposes them gradually to the harsh reality of their loss. Numbness tempers the chill and softens the sadness to the point where these feelings can be endured. It does this by raising the bereaved's threshold against recognition of reality and muting the full emotional impact of the loss.

The numbness is also a buffer that makes it possible to do what must be done in the immediate aftermath of a great personal loss: making arrangements, taking care of daily needs, getting through the funeral or memorial service. Some people are so protected by this sensation that they manage to cope with stunning efficiency, apparently disconnected from the explosion of pain deep inside. Although they may experience the numbness as a sense of unreality and a feeling of emotional distance from other people, it actually temporarily supports them. This period may last from a few days to a few weeks, with alternating times of "normal" behavior and moments of despair and anguish as the full reality of the loss briefly penetrates into their consciousness. Inability to think clearly, restlessness, and confusion may accompany these times.

During this phase of disbelief and numbness the bereaved may seem relatively unaffected, even surprisingly accepting of the loss. The key word is *seem.* As a condoler, you need to understand that this behavior is one natural face of grief in the early stages. Over the next few weeks, as waves of emotional turmoil surface, a more recognizable manifestation of grief is likely to emerge. Numbness is replaced by a roller coaster of emotions. Time and talk and tears are the bereaved's allies.

In subtle forms, denial and numbness often return intermittently for months and may manifest themselves in very disconcerting ways. Emily Dickinson captures this phenomenon most poetically:

> The distance that the dead have gone
> Does not at first appear
> Their coming back seems possible
> For many an ardent year.

The bereaved may "see" their loved one in a crowd only to draw near and find a stranger. They may "hear" the sound of the deceased's footsteps or even their voice or find themselves setting an extra place at the dinner table. Such experiences are fleeting glimpses of the mind's desire to deny reality. Death is acknowledged first by the mind and only later fully accepted by the heart. C. S. Lewis wrote about this unique frustration in his book, *A Grief Observed* (1961), an eloquent journal written following the death of his wife: "I think I am beginning to understand why grief feels like suspense. It comes from the frustration of so many impulses that had become habitual. . . . Now their target is gone. I keep on, through habit, fitting an arrow to the string; then I remember and I have to lay the bow down. . . . So many roads once; now so many culs-de-sac" (p. 55).

Experiencing the Pain

When William Butler Yeats wrote, "Things fall apart, the center cannot hold," he wasn't speaking of the second phase of grief, but the line aptly describes the sense of chaos that prevails when numbness starts to fade. It's when grief reaches the heart that the real pain begins. Within hours to days after the death, this second phase is felt. The numbness may linger, but the reality of the loss begins, more and more, to manifest itself in the outward signs of inner grief. Disbelief eventually gives way to belief; numbness gives way to feeling. This natural progression pushes the bereaved forward into painful sensations and reality. The bubbling cauldron of emotions that has been held in check begins to boil over, sometimes with frightening intensity. For many in grief it seems nearly impossible to keep things in control. Shakespeare wrote, "Our griefs, not our manners, reason now."

Anguish and suffering may now affect all aspects of the bereaved's life, from emotional swings to physical problems, from confused thinking to what seem to be strange changes in behavior. It's as if the ground, once so familiar, is no longer there to support the bereaved—in part because those things that were most meaningful when the deceased were alive often become the most painful now that they are gone.

Perhaps the most unique features of grief are *pining* and *searching*. Pining is the compelling and soulful longing for the deceased. Searching is the powerful unconscious urge to find a "lost" love. Both are experienced in such uncanny ways that the edges of the bereaved's contact with reality may temporarily blur. The mourners yearn to re-create, to recover their loved one, while knowing, intellectually at least, that the yearning is futile.

For most, this puzzling experience is disorienting, even maddening, and there will be moments when the grieving person's inner wish to deny reality is stronger than their acceptance. At times their loved one may seem everywhere palpable. Familiar surroundings yield unending reminders and trigger misperceptions that are a natural part of this phenomenon. Your bereaved friends may "see" their lost loved one in the faces of others or "hear" the deceased, either by misinterpreting a spoken voice or "hearing" the voice "out of nowhere." They may sense the loved one's presence, even "feel" the touch of a familiar hand.

Occasionally, those in mourning temporarily take on some of the traits of their deceased loved one. For example, you may notice them repeating a phrase the deceased often said. The bereaved may deliberately do things that stimulate memories, like going to a special restaurant or watching a favorite film repeatedly. On the other hand, and equally "normal," don't be surprised if the bereaved's behavior is, for a time, geared to avoiding situations that trigger recollections. Unsettling as all these occurrences may sometimes be, you may assure the bereaved that when these behaviors no longer serve a useful purpose, they will disappear.

This second phase of grief, experiencing the pain, is not only associated with pining and searching but has four other threads that when woven together form the fabric of mourning. They are physical complaints, emotional swings, thinking disturbances, and changes in behavior.

Physical complaints associated with distress come in waves. They include shortness of breath, tightness in the throat, sighing, feelings of emptiness in the stomach, a nearly overwhelming weakness, and headaches. Appetite may diminish or even disappear for a time. Occasionally, appetite will increase, particularly if eating in the past has provided emotional comfort. Sleep may be fretful with disturbing dreams, and middle-of-the-night or early-morning awakening can leave the bereaved feeling exhausted, anxious, and tense. Periods of aimless, exhausted inactivity are shot through with bursts of sharp-edged energy. The bereaved may experience the entire spectrum of these sensations at different times.

These physical disturbances are often intermittent and usually clear up naturally over the weeks and months ahead. However, if the physical complaints are troubling or persistent, don't assume that they are the product of grief. As a condoling friend, you might suggest that the bereaved see their physician just to be sure.

Emotional swings are likely to be a part of daily life no matter how desperately those in grief want to stay in control. When the numbness and disbelief begin to give way, an unfocused anxiety can show itself in restlessness and tension. The bereaved may feel so tense that they are unable to sit in one spot for long. They may pace endlessly or be unable to go to sleep. This anxiety can be unrelenting or may come and go, but in any case, four strong emotions begin to be apparent: fear, sadness, anger, and guilt. During this phase these feelings are intertwined in endless and often troubling patterns.

Out of anxiety may come nameless *fears* or moments of panic, apparently without cause. Fear of dying or of having other loved ones suddenly die are not uncommon. Fear of being alone or of going outside can be embarrassing and very disabling. All these fears come and go without warning, and it's the unpredictability that's so devastating.

The *sadness* of loss is often the most all-consuming feeling of emptiness ever experienced. Hopelessness and helplessness spill forth at unexpected times. It seems impossible for the bereaved to enjoy anything or anyone. Life appears hollow and the despair seems unending.

Even those who ordinarily don't cry may now find tears flowing, and with them may come comfort. Shakespeare, whose insights on grief are extraordinary, wrote, "Now is that noble vessel full of grief, that runs it over even at his eyes." While sometimes anticipated, tears can be triggered by untimely events in unlikely places. Some bereaved people report that at isolated moments, in the shower or preparing a meal, they suddenly find themselves crying like a helpless child. They may begin to cry while shopping for groceries, talking to a neighbor, or in the middle of a business meeting. Embarrassed, they may feel they owe others an apology. You might gently remind the bereaved that grief is one situation in which the tears of an adult are generally accepted and understood. No excuses are needed. Of course, some adults rarely cry and even deeply felt grief may not trigger tears in these mourners. If tears do come, encourage the bereaved to allow them; they help the healing process.

Frustration, helplessness, and insecurity often lead to irritability and *anger*. Anger may be rational and focused, as in a death caused by a drunk driver, or it may seem irrational and illogical, as after a natural death. The bereaved may strike out at family, friends, physicians, clergy, employers, and employees, virtually anyone and everyone, including God.

There is no better evidence for the irrationality of this anger than the fact that it is sometimes directed toward the lost loved one. But those in grief *are* angry; they often feel abandoned. Such losses touch deep memories of childhood when we were first left alone. The death of a loved one also forces a confrontation with one's own mortality. Again, anger may result. Feelings of irritability, bitterness, hostility, and aggression are often so surprising that the mourners may fear themselves on the verge of a breakdown. But anger is another important part of the healing process. Through its reasonable expression, powerful energies are released.

Guilt can also be tremendously disabling. It erodes self-esteem and evokes self-condemnation. While pangs of guilt may be natural, it's destructive to hold on to such feelings. If guilt is not resolved, the healing cannot be completed.

Initially, the bereaved may feel guilty because they seem unable to cope as well as they think they should in the aftermath of the death. Or guilt may be experienced in response to feelings of anger toward their loved one for dying. It may also arise upon recognition of unconscious death wishes they may have felt toward the deceased, as in the case of a long illness. Surprisingly, the pain of guilt is also a natural response when those who have traveled the long path of grief first begin to feel happy again.

There's another kind of guilt that arises out of the very normal ambivalence that is present even in the deepest love relationships. In *Necessary Losses,* Judith Viorst says, "We saw them as less than perfect and we loved them less than perfectly." After the death of a loved one, the bereaved may dwell on areas of regret such as, "I should have been more understanding" and the infamous "If only. . . ." There's always some nasty word that can't be forgotten, some fight that can never be made up. Quarrels or episodes of selfishness are recalled through the pain of guilt.

Amazingly enough, all these emotions, often so difficult in the experiencing, are effective and practical responses to loss. They serve to ensure the survival of the bereaved by assisting in the process of readjustment. From this perspective, we can see that anxiety serves to mobilize energy for the tasks at hand. The four emotions that follow—fear, sadness, anger, and guilt—have important functions, too. Fear of being alone is one of the motivating factors behind recommitment to relationships with others. And it is during the painful emotion of sadness that those in grief are most likely to redefine their priorities, goals, and sense of purpose. Guilt is directed toward oneself and anger is directed toward others, but both have similar functions. Each provokes the bereaved to reassess their sense of fairness and justice.

The emotional roller coaster is one thing; *lapses in clear thinking* are another. The bereaved may be disconcerted by poor concentration, slowness in thinking, and problems with memory. This last area ranges from simple day-to-day forgetfulness to losing one's train of thought or encountering memory blocks. The most terrifying notion, of course, is the fear of forgetting the deceased. We guarantee it won't happen. Grieving has no permanent effect on memory. However, if you're close to the bereaved, you may want to caution them against making impulsive decisions. If there are major choices to be made early in grief, it's wise to wait to finalize them.

Bereavement is also associated with *changes in behavior* that encompass both relationships with others and day-to-day activities. Usual health habits, housekeeping chores, and work routines may be in disarray. To those in grief, the simplest activities such as paying bills and running errands often feel like major burdens for a while. They may wander about the house aimlessly, picking up things and putting them down, or just staring into space. Periods of despair may cause them to throw caution to the wind in an effort to put off painful sensations. You may observe them compromising their health with excessive drinking and poor eating and hygiene habits. A few may be prone to take foolish risks such as reckless driving, spending money inappropriately, or giving away precious possessions indiscriminately.

Imagine how all these changes might affect one's sense of self. You may provide enormous comfort by assuring and reassuring the bereaved that feelings of "falling apart" are not at all uncommon for those experiencing profound loss. By now this must seem like an unending refrain, but it's true:

These sensations are natural, they serve a purpose, and they will subside in time.

RESOLUTION AND ACCEPTANCE

There's a tendency among many well-meaning people to expect those in grief to work through their sorrow in a period of weeks, but there is no timetable for this extraordinary process. The human heart does not obey the rules of logic. Each of us is unique, has diverse inner resources, and heals at a different rate. Throughout their days the bereaved are likely to experience moments of grief prompted by things as simple as a remembered ritual, a much-loved item of clothing, a face, an anniversary, a familiar scene. The raw pain of loss will emerge as a reminder of the time that once was.

Although most bereaved are able to resume their daily routine with relatively normal functioning in a few weeks or months, it often takes much longer before they truly begin to turn to the future and make some peace with the past. Life may still be strongly influenced by loss a year and a half to three years later, when the final phase of healing resolves.

One of the greatest barriers to healing is the understandable fact that many people try to avoid the intense distress connected with the grief experience and to avoid the expression of emotions associated with it. Allowing the anguish of baseless guilt, objectless rage, disabling loneliness, and fears of madness is a challenge for even the most stable. However, as grief gradually loses its potency, the pain and struggle diminish. No longer something to be contained, grief is usually, if surprisingly, transformed into something that can be appreciated as part of the totality of life's experience.

Deep grief is so universal and painful a phenomenon that we repeatedly forget how wondrous a healing process it is. Its duration seems in great part to depend on the success with which the bereaved allow the suffering, that is, does the "grief" work. But at some point, a turn in the road *will* be felt. It may be the first laugh or the moment the bereaved realize that they're beginning to think about those who have faced similar heartbreaks.

There are five primary goals or tasks in the grief process. Although these are interwoven and not necessarily accomplished sequentially, we'll talk about them one by one.

First: Accepting the finality of the loss. It may seem simple, but it is a highly complex process. The urge to deny is so powerful that it often blurs the harshness of reality. Addressing this issue in his book *Grief Counseling and Grief Therapy*, J. William Worden says "Part of the acceptance of reality is to come to the belief that reunion is impossible, at least in this life" (p. 11). The mind can accept things long before the heart, so it's easy for the bereaved to believe that acceptance has occurred, when in fact the realization has only just begun to touch the core of their being. Acceptance is gradual and comes in waves; denial is ready and waiting as a friend to help protect the mourner from emotional overload.

Second: Accepting the painful thoughts, feelings, and behaviors that are so much a part of mourning. As hard as it is, the bereaved need to allow the pain and anguish of their suffering to take place. Healing is hampered by resisting the process and suppressing natural expressions of grief. Rather than fighting these emotional tides, the bereaved will be best served if they allow themselves to be washed by the waves of sadness. It's as if they are standing at the water's edge, bracing themselves for the onslaught of an engulfing wave. A little give in the knees is needed. Pushing away at the waves won't help.

Third: Redirecting the loving energy once focused on the lost relationship. With the death of a loved one, an immense void opens. In order to fill that void, the mourners must first let go, and then reclaim the energy that once bound them to the loved one. Finally, the bereaved will be able to reorient this loving energy toward new relationships. It is not easy. Some find the letting go so painful that they promise themselves never to love again. In addition, many in grief experience some guilt and shame when they first become aware that they are feeling affection for someone new. Others recovering from grief are afraid that in reclaiming a place for themselves in the world they dishonor the memory of their past relationship. Healing involves recognizing that those in grief honor both themselves and their loved ones by living fully once again.

Fourth: Reviewing and crystallizing memories of the deceased loved one. Loss precipitates remembrance. The death of a loved one breaks a psychological dam. Early in grief, images, events, situations, bits of conversation, and fragments of feelings flood the bereaved's mind. Initially, this deluge of memories may seem overwhelming. Whenever we feel out of control, fear and helplessness surface. Throughout the process of grief, aspects of this review return. It's not only that certain things bring loss to mind; it's that there are times when nearly everything the bereaved hear, see, taste, touch, and recall causes them to dwell on their loss. It is painful, but again, it's important since the mind searches the past in an effort to make sense of the experience. Through this part of the healing process, those in grief come to better understand the nature of their relationship and what exactly it was that was lost.

Typically, the initial mental images are beautiful ones, devoid of negative or undesirable features. These act as healing buffers and serve to cushion feelings of regret, guilt, and anger at a time when the bereaved have little ability to cope. In the natural progression of healing, this review eventually becomes more realistic and balanced, containing both positive and negative recollections. Gradually, an image of life with the deceased is created. In a sense, the bereaved are consciously and unconsciously choosing "photographs" for a very personal internal souvenir album. Theirs will not be the only memories to find their way into this cherished collection. Condolers can add by sharing their memories of the deceased.

Fifth: Selecting memories to incorporate into the fabric of the bereaved's life. It's like weaving a silver thread into a silk cloth;

the thread is so fine and the crafting is so beautifully done that one scarcely sees it. Strangely, one may unite with their loved one in death in a way that is rarely possible in life. "Remembrance is a form of meeting," says the poet Gibran.

No one who has suffered a profound loss will ever be the same. The bereaved may become a different self or even a better self, but they will never regain their previous identity. Through the process of remembering, reexperiencing, and integrating, those in grief are transformed. Emergence from the loss of a close loved one involves a panoramic adaptation including changes in behavior, self-perception, and expectations.

The bereaved show clear indications when the healing work is done: the ability to remember, without anguish, both the joys and the disappointments of the lost relationship; a wholehearted return to regular activities; and the reorienting of energies to one's new life. There will probably be a fragrance of sorrow when the bereaved thinks of the deceased, but the sorrow will have a different quality, more like a tender longing than a hole in one's heart. A time will arrive when the notion of "getting through the day" ceases. As one bereaved woman wrote to a friend quoting Albert Camus, "In the midst of winter, I finally learned that there was in me an invincible summer."

Chapter 3

Attachment and Loss

Why does the death of someone we care about hurt so much? One of the great paradoxes of life is that in our very capacity to form bonds with others, we carry the seeds for suffering when those relationships are over.

From the time we are young and our first friend moves away, we begin to recognize that loss is part of living. As social beings, our very existence depends on attachment to others. Yet, every human relationship is destined to end in loss. Endings are the price paid for having beginnings and, except for the loss of one's own life, the death of a loved one is the ultimate loss.

THE TIES THAT BIND

What is this phenomenon called attachment, this fundamental need for human connection? The British psychoanalyst, John Bowlby, has focused his professional work on unraveling the mysteries of attachment: how it affects our lives and influences our behavior. His thesis is that attachments begin in infancy and continue through life because as social beings we're more likely to survive with others around us. Early attachments are created most frequently through closeness to parents or primary caregivers. Thus, the fear and anger that later come with separation derive from the literal truth that without a protecting caretaker we as infants were less likely to survive. Herein lies the lesson of loss. Denial, protest, fear, anger, searching, crying, and other responses to the loss of a loved one have their source in deep-rooted perceptions that our safety may be threatened. Similar stages were first mapped by psychiatrist Elisabeth Kübler-Ross, who explored the emotional shifts in dying patients.

A small boy lost on the beach doesn't intellectually reason that finding his mother is advantageous for his physical survival. All he knows is that he wants and needs her and she's not there. His tears and cries are based in this primitive attachment response; he feels a deep pang and a desperate urge to search and find her. His spontaneous crying and calling have great "survival" value in alerting his mother to his location.

Some animals and birds display similar behavior in response to separation or death. One poignant description comes from *On Aggression* by Konrad Lorenz, Ph.D., who observed the behavior of a goose parted from its mate:

> The first response to the disappearance of the partner consists in the anxious attempt to find him again. The goose moves about restlessly by day and night, flying great distances and visiting places where the partner might be found, uttering all the time the penetrating . . . call. The searching expeditions are extended farther and farther.

Much of the behavior associated with grief is rooted in a deep survival instinct. Its primary purpose is to "regain" the lost person. Consider, again, the little boy separated from his mother on a crowded beach. His crying and calling work! He is reunited with his mother.

Behaviors such as his, unconscious as they are, are "designed" for situations where reuniting is possible. However, in an irrecoverable loss such as death, similar behaviors are seen on the part of those in grief. We cry in disbelief; we protest in anger; we call out in hope that our loved one will return. It is as if our heart and mind cannot tell the difference between temporary separation and permanent loss.

THE MINI-GRIEF RESPONSE

The first challenge in understanding grief is to understand loss. The first lesson of loss is that no change or growth can occur without it. Exits and entrances are an integral part of life.

The interdependence of greeting and parting, beginnings and endings, attachment and loss is basic to all life processes. Innumerable little good-byes or "mini-grief responses" are experienced as the years unfold. An old English proverb says, "No day passeth without some little griefs." Youth is lost; possessions are lost. Jobs, military service, travel, and new relationships take us away from significant persons in our life. Changes in attitudes, beliefs, and even ambitions are indeed small deaths. Divorce, desertion, separation, and rejection mean coping with profound loss. Illness, accidents, and aging can transform a loved one, sometimes so drastically that the person we once knew seems lost to us. Whenever we go through a separation or significant loss, uncertainty is likely to be part of this transition. We may feel that change should become substantially easier as we mature, but for most, resistance to change is natural and predictable.

We should not be surprised that each undesired loss, whether the termination of a relationship or the loss of a wallet, produces some sort of grief reaction. While less intense, these mini-grief responses follow similar patterns to those an actual death can set in motion. Such mini-grief responses help teach us about letting go.

Consider your reaction to the loss of a wallet. Suppose that you've taken the kids to a Saturday matinee. One of them asks for popcorn. You reach for your wallet. It's gone! Your first response? "Oh, no!" You reach into your other pockets, fumbling through your coat. You search around the floor with your foot. Distracted and unable to focus on the movie, you begin to review where it might be. The concession counter? The street? Your last stop at the gas station? The pleasure of the afternoon is replaced with anxiety. You feel guilty for not being more careful, and a little angry, too. You may even find yourself directing some of that anger at your kids for having "created" the problem—after all, you went to the movies for them. Preoccupied with thoughts of what you'll need to do next, you feel restless. And on it goes. Eventually, even if you never locate the wallet, you will come to terms with the loss, perhaps even learning something from it.

Here, then, is grief in miniature: a touch of shock, a bit of denial, searching behavior, a sprinkle of anxiety, sadness, anger and guilt, preoccupation, then a review before accepting and letting go.

The psychiatrist and renowned grief expert, Dr. Colin Murray Parkes, points out in *Bereavement* that:

> In the ongoing flux of life human beings undergo many changes . . . every change involves a loss and a gain . . . individuals are faced with the need to give up one mode of life and accept another. If they identify the change as a gain, acceptance may not be hard, but when it is a loss . . . they will do their best to resist the change. Resistance to change, the reluctance to give up possessions, people, status, expectation—this, I believe, is the basis of grief. (p. 30)

In the course of maturing, there is continued confrontation with the experience of separation and loss. Out of this pattern of endless coping with partings, our attitudes are shaped. Each moment is lost to the next, yet each moment is the foundation on which the next is born.

The drama of human contact is played on many stages and each of us is one of the countless players. The cast includes everyone we know plus all sorts of people as yet unknown to us. Routinely, we meet, relate, and part—often fleetingly—with a variety of emotions. The drama of comings and goings never ends. Every separation, every parting, is a kind of dying; every loss is a kind of death, a series of endless lessons and challenges, opportunities to fully face the ultimate challenge of living and dying. Each person brings to any major loss a backlog of experience in dealing with innumerable prior small losses. This background leaves the person relatively prepared or unprepared, competent or incompetent, to cope effectively with a current loss.

Part II

What Can I Write?

When President Abraham Lincoln was informed that Mrs. Lydia Bixby had lost five sons fighting for the Union in the Civil War, he wrote this, perhaps the most famous of all condolence letters.

Dear Madam,

I have been shown in the files of the War Department a statement of the Adjutant General of Massachusetts that you are the mother of five sons who have died gloriously on the field of battle. I feel how weak and fruitless must be any word of mine which should attempt to beguile you from the grief of a loss so overwhelming. But I cannot refrain from tendering you the consolation that may be found in the thanks of the republic they died to save. I pray that our Heavenly Father may assuage the anguish of your bereavement, and leave you only the cherished memory of the loved and lost, and the solemn pride that must be yours to have laid so costly a sacrifice upon the altar of freedom.

Yours very sincerely and respectfully,

A. Lincoln

Chapter 4

Getting Started

THE MOST DIFFICULT LETTER OF ALL

There is no doubt about it! The most challenging letter an individual is ever called upon to write is a letter of condolence. How do you convey on paper your message of comfort and compassion? How do you fashion a net of words to help sustain and support someone as they fall through the pain and turmoil of grief? Even though you may call, send flowers or a telegram, or attend the memorial service, none of these actions takes the place of writing a letter to someone whose bereavement has touched your heart.

The written word often brings great comfort when an individual is coping with loss. Many letters of condolence are cherished and saved for years. A friend wrote to us of his appreciation for letters received upon the death of his wife several years ago:

> After reading them the first time, I put the letters aside in a shoe box, fully intending to reread them in a month or two. I stalled for fear that they would rekindle my deep sadness. Now, nearly six years after my wife's death, I read them afresh with an open heart. There are horrible pangs, of course, but it's not my pain the letters renew, it's the tender and loving memories—not only of my wife, but of those many caring friends who committed their feelings to paper.

To say in a few appropriate words what we deeply feel may seem awkward. While we wish to express our sympathy and acknowledge grief, we want to avoid being superficial, flowery, or contrived. To write a meaningful message in a few paragraphs is often a challenge that becomes a chore. Unfortunately, this discomfort causes many people, despite their caring feelings, not to write at all.

It shouldn't be difficult to write a good letter of condolence if you are genuinely moved to sympathy by another's loss. It shouldn't be difficult to write with kindness and understanding if you feel someone's grief and share in the tragic impact of it. Still, responding to a basic human impulse, we grope for words that will bring solace and we find it difficult to say what will rightly express our feelings.

So often we experience profound moments both in writing and reading a letter of condolence. For the writer, these moments frequently occur as feelings of compassion are transformed into words. For the bereaved, who is reading your letter at a time of vulnerability, the world may be experienced in a totally new way. A letter of condolence provides the opportunity for a very special form of writer/reader interconnection, one that proclaims, simply, "I acknowledge your loss, and, in some measure, I share your pain." This is the essential human message in all letters of condolence.

HOW TO BEGIN

In the pages that follow are practical guidelines that will help you transform the challenge of writing a letter of condolence into a positive and creative process. Depending on your individual needs and skills, you may wish to proceed in one of four ways.

1. *Compose an original letter.* If you want to craft your own letter, Chapter 5 offers a set of seven simple and clear guidelines to assist in your writing.

2. *Modify and personalize an existing letter or letters.* For some writers, an existing letter may so totally suit their feelings, style, and tone that they wish to use it and make appropriate

alterations. The chapters in Part III address some of the special concerns the bereaved might have following specific losses (e.g., the death of a spouse, the death of a child). Each section concludes with a selection of well-written sample letters.

3. *Choose a quotation, reading, or historic letter to speak for you, adding a personal note.* Many bereaved have told us that they were particularly touched when condoling friends included with their sympathy note a poem, reading, or copy of a historic letter. The section entitled "Quotations Through Time" at the end of this book may provide ideas. Beautiful historic letters can be found throughout Part III.

4. *You may prefer to express your sympathy through a commercial condolence card or telegram* (refer to Chapter 6).

ETIQUETTE

Most comprehensive books on grief, letter writing, and etiquette do not include quality guidance on condolence letters. (Much of this material seems more intent on commiserating with the reader over "what a difficult task it is" than in providing assistance in composing a meaningful letter.) Of course, there is no "right" way of expressing sympathy through the written word. There are, however, a few helpful rules of etiquette that have evolved through social tradition.

1. *To whom does one write?*

A letter of condolence is most often written to the bereaved person with whom you have had the closest relationship. If you knew the deceased well, but do not know members of the surviving family, it is still a gracious gesture to write a condolence letter. In writing to a married person who has lost a parent, you may write to the one whose parent died, or, if the other partner was close to the deceased, the letter may be addressed to both.

Surviving children who have lost either a parent, grandparent, or sibling are often overlooked in letters of condolence. Acknowledging their grief with either specific mention of their name in a letter to the family or a personal note addressed to the child is thoughtful and important.

Should a letter of condolence be written to the surviving member of a divorced couple when the former spouse dies? In many instances, yes. If the couple has maintained a friendly relationship since the divorce, a letter is likely to be appreciated. If in doubt, write.

2. *What time frame is appropriate?*

Write promptly upon hearing the news. It is best not to wait for the shock to wear off, and do not use the excuse of waiting for the "right words" to come. If you write while your heart is full, your letter will be far more likely to express, in a natural way, the sincere sympathy you feel. Every effort should be made to send letters of condolence within two weeks of your learning of the death. Consider six weeks the outside limit of appropriateness for most situations.

On occasion, we have been asked if it is acceptable to send a letter of condolence months or even years after a death. This question typically comes from individuals who have experienced a pang over what they felt to be "unfinished business." Such persons hesitate to write after a long period both out of embarrassment and for fear of rekindling grief in the bereaved.

Our response is simple. Genuine expressions of sympathy change in their impact over time, but they are always appropriate. If you neglected to write at the time of the death but wish to do so now, follow your feelings. You needn't apologize. However, don't use this atypical circumstance as an excuse to avoid writing immediately following a death.

3. *What kind of stationery is appropriate?*

Any standard stationery is suitable, but typical colors include white, gray, cream, or pastels. Personalized stationery is also appropriate. Bold patterns and colors generally should be avoided.

Although not required, traditionally, letters of condolence

are handwritten, especially by close friends. A handwritten letter of condolence lends a warm touch that is more personal. Government and business organizations usually have their letters typed, and this is acceptable. For more information about letters from professionals and organizations, see Chapter 9.

4. *How long should the letter be?*

Expressions of sympathy are not measured by the number of words used, so length should not be a major consideration. Some etiquette books strongly encourage brevity, but this is based on the incorrect assumption that those in grief are not interested in reading a lengthy letter. (For many bereaved, this is not the case.) The guidelines presented in this book suggest a minimum of four components in the sympathy note and seven in the complete letter of condolence, but keep in mind that these guidelines are only suggestions. Following these guidelines, your letter may range from a few sentences to a few pages.

WORDS OF CAUTION

One of the reasons we sometimes hesitate to write a letter of condolence is that we don't want to say the wrong thing. It is indeed possible! For example, a writer's own fears, needs, and desires may lead him or her to become inappropriately invested in the bereaved's quick recovery. This may cause the writer to use expressions that are experienced by the bereaved as insensitive rather than comforting. Cool or inappropriate words may also reflect the writer's fear of being relied on for help in this difficult time. In well-meaning efforts to condole, whether in writing or through the spoken word, a number of phrases may more often affront than console. For example: "Don't cry; try to keep control of yourself." "You're young; there's plenty of time to have other children." "I know exactly what you are going through." A more extensive discussion of phrases to avoid is found in Chapter 12.

Just get started! Remember that your letter or note of condolence is a message of compassion. One of the thousands of letters written by the eighteenth-century English author, William Cowper, began with this bit of advice:

> When one has a Letter to write there is nothing more useful than to make a Beginning. In the first place, because unless it be begun, there is no good reason to hope that it will ever be ended, and secondly, because the beginning is half the business, it being much more difficult to put the pen in motion at first, than to continue the progress of it, when once moved.

Chapter 5

Guidelines for Composing Letters and Notes of Condolence

A thoughtful letter of condolence is both a tribute to the deceased and a source of comfort and courage to the living. The guidelines that follow are not presented as a set of rigid rules; rather, they are offered as suggestions for transforming your feelings, concerns, sympathy, and love into meaningful written communication. Many people have told us that they reread letters of condolence again and again, days, months, and even years after the loss. Some even pass these letters down through the family for generations. A sensitive letter of condolence is not only an enduring consolation but it is an enduring conversation.

Unfortunately, many people miss the essence of good letter writing when they sit down to begin. They find it difficult to express themselves in a simple, natural way; instead, they think they must write "better" than they speak. In an effort to be literary and correct they sound affected and lose the quality of personal sincerity. Generally, with the exception of a business letter of condolence, writers should make every effort to write as if they were speaking with the bereaved. A good letter is like a visit on paper. Use your usual vocabulary and phrasing. Ideally, the person who receives your letter should almost be able to see and hear you while reading it.

After studying thousands of condolence letters and analyzing their structure, we have identified seven key components.

While many beautiful and profound letters of condolence do not contain all seven components, or use them in a different sequence, understanding these components provides the writer with a practical, simple, and clear outline. The order of the components is not carved in stone; however, the order presented here is that most frequently noted. This set of seven guidelines applies specifically to instances when you knew the deceased. An example is presented on page 40 for those situations where you know only the bereaved and not the person who died.

LETTERS: THE SEVEN COMPONENTS

1. *Acknowledge the loss.* If you have been informed of the death by a source other than the person to whom you are writing, note how you came to learn of the news. Here it is perfectly appropriate to relate one's shock and dismay at hearing about the loss. This acknowledgment immediately sets clear the purpose and tone of the letter. No matter what the circumstance, it is always advisable in your letter to mention the deceased by name.

2. *Express your sympathy.* Express your sorrow sincerely. In sending your words of sympathy, you let the grieving persons know that you care and that, in some way, you relate to the anguish of their loss. Be honest; don't hesitate to use the word *death* or note the actual cause of death, even suicide. If you knew the person who died, which of course is not always the case, by sharing your own sadness you support the bereaved and remind them that they are not completely alone in their suffering.

3. *Note special qualities of the deceased.* Take a moment to acknowledge those characteristics you cherished most about the deceased. These may be specific attributes such as a keen wit, generous nature, or love of sports. They may be personality characteristics, for example, courage, leadership, or decisiveness. They may be ways in which the individual related

to the world, as through religious devotion or community service. When you recount such qualities, you help remind the bereaved that their loved one was appreciated by others. If you didn't know the deceased personally, you may wish to recount qualities you have heard about.

4. *Recount a memory about the deceased.* Early in bereavement, memories of the deceased are often temporarily dimmed. This can be frightening for those in grief. Relate a brief, memorable anecdote or two. In the recounting, try to capture what it was about the deceased that evoked your appreciation, affection, or respect. You may wish to say a few words about how he or she touched and influenced your life. And don't avoid humorous incidents; they can be most appropriate and very gratefully received. Laughter is a great healer.

5. *Note special qualities of the bereaved.* The loss of a loved one can be so overwhelming that strong feelings of inadequacy surface and the bereaved may feel shaky about even their most basic abilities. They typically experience at least a transitory impairment in their usual capacity for self-appreciation and self-love. This is a time when even the most courageous individuals will appreciate your reminding them of their personal strengths, especially those qualities that will help them through this period. These may be traits that you know served them through adversity in the past such as resilience, patience, competence, religious devotion, optimism, or a trusting nature. This can be beautifully amplified if you recall a loving remark about the survivor that was once made by the deceased.

6. *Offer assistance.* Many, but not all, sympathy letters include an offer to help. If you sincerely wish to offer your assistance, do so, but if you choose not to, you can still write a beautiful condolence letter. If you decide to offer help, keep in mind that the standard, "Let me know if there is anything I can do," may put a burden on the grieving individual to ask you for assistance. Although a *general* offer to help is not out of line, a more sensitive approach reflecting

your sincere desire to be of help is to make a *specific* offer (doing the grocery shopping, running errands, answering the phone, taking care of the children, helping with correspondence). Those in the numbness of early grief can often scarcely hear the well-meant "Is there anything I can do?" let alone summon up a vision of what actually needs to be done. More suggestions for specific ways to help can be found in Part V. Your caring sentiment and genuine offer to help may be more readily accepted if you are willing to take the initiative. Once having made an offer, be sure to follow through on your promise.

7. *Close with a thoughtful word or phrase.* The closing in a letter of condolence can be particularly significant. Let your concluding words reflect the truth of your feelings. Is it "love," "fondly," "yours truly," "sincerely," or would you prefer to close with a phrase or sentence that reiterates your sympathy? For example:

My affectionate respects to you and yours.

Our love is with you always.

You are in my thoughts and prayers.

You know you have my deepest sympathy and my love and friendship always.

My heart and my tears are with you.

We share in your grief and send you our love.

We offer our affectionate sympathy and many beautiful memories.

My thoughts are with you now, and I send you my deepest sympathy.

We all join in sending you our heartfelt love.

WHEN YOU KNEW THE DECEASED

The following letter illustrates the seven components just discussed. In this case, the writer knows both the bereaved and the deceased.

A Complete Letter of Condolence: Example 1

Dear Keith,

1. **Acknowledge the loss.**

   My heart ached when Tim called this morning and I heard the news of Ruth's death. Though not unexpected, the final word was still felt as a blow.

2. **Express your sympathy.**

   Words seem so inadequate, but with this letter comes my heart filled with love and sympathy on the loss of your beloved wife. I loved her too.

3. **Note special qualities of the deceased.**

   Ruth was a vibrant, talented, caring woman and dearly loved by everyone whose life she touched. But for me, she was even more. She was a rare and cherished friend. Through our friendship, my vision of the beauty and possibilities of life grew.

4. **Recount a memory about the deceased.**

   As I write, flooded with precious memories, I am recalling the day when Ruth and I were driving to the coast for what we thought would be a lazy afternoon of beachcombing. Instead, we had a flat tire. You've never seen a pair of more fumble-fingered, grease-covered, laughing clowns than we were that day, but we did it! And we made it to the beach just in time for a glorious sunset.

5. **Note special qualities of the bereaved.**

   I know you will miss her deeply, but I also know that you recognize the blessings of the beautiful years you shared. You were always a source of strength and courage to Ruth. I recall her once saying that your love of life and enduring optimism brought her closer to God. I trust these same qualities will help support and guide you during this oh-so-difficult time.

6. **Offer assistance.**

   You know you have my sympathy and my friendship, and I would be grateful if you would turn to me for any help I might give. I'll call this weekend to see if there's anything I can do.

7. Close with a thoughtful word or phrase.

My prayers and thoughts are with you.

WHEN YOU DIDN'T KNOW THE PERSON WHO DIED

Of course, the form of your letter will in large part be governed by whether you knew the deceased. Particularly as we get older and our circle of social and professional acquaintances widens, occasions arise when we are moved to write a letter about the loss of someone we never knew. For example, you may wish to write to a business associate following the death of one of his or her parents whom you never met. In addition, two less frequent circumstances arise (1) if you knew the deceased but never met the person to whom you are writing, and (2) if you have met neither the bereaved nor the deceased, as in a letter concerning the death of a famous person. Any letter may be written by adapting these guidelines.

A COMPLETE LETTER OF CONDOLENCE: EXAMPLE 2

Dear Ellen,

1. Acknowledge the loss.

This morning Mr. Moore told us the sad news of your father's sudden death.

2. Express your sympathy.

Let me first extend my heartfelt sympathy to you and your family. The loss must touch you very deeply as you face these first numbing days of grief.

3. Note special qualities of the deceased.

4. Recount a memory about the deceased.

(*Note:* These two components may not apply if you never met the deceased. However, it can be quite meaningful to the bereaved if you are able to recall any special qualities or memories they may have shared with you in the past about their loved one.)

Though I never met your Dad, I remember how touched I was when you described the scene as he recited a poem he'd composed for your mother at their fiftieth wedding anniversary celebration last year. His tenderness and humor were both captured in that story as was your obvious love for him.

5. **Note special qualities of the bereaved.**

   While our relationship has been largely in the office, I have seen you handle challenging situations for the firm time and again. During this difficult period, I know you will draw on these same deep personal resources so many of us have come to respect and admire.

6. **Offer assistance.**

   During your absence, Dan and I will cover your accounts—maybe not with your finesse, but with as much savvy as we can muster. We've had a terrific mentor.

7. **Close with a thoughtful word or phrase.**

   Keep in mind that this office is filled with people who care about you and are thinking about you in your sorrow.

THREE ADDITIONAL OPTIONS

Three additional components may be incorporated in a letter of condolence. These options are found frequently in the letters we have reviewed, but not as often as the seven basic components. Although they are seen less often, they have the potential to add rich, inspirational, and comforting dimensions to a letter of condolence.

1. *Share your philosophy of life or provide a religious commentary.*

Death almost always brings in its wake a renewed awareness and reawakening of our spiritual beliefs. If you choose to use references to religion in your letter of condolence, be sensitive to the religious orientation of the bereaved. It would be most unusual, however, to offend anyone by offering your prayers as a personal act of love. Discrepancies of religious belief matter little if your effort to console is an authentic one and your espousal of beliefs is not strongly contrary to those of the bereaved.

Obviously you should not use the occasion to try to convert the bereaved to a particular point of view, but feel free to express yourself in religious terms if these are the words that come to you naturally. All responses to the loss of a loved one raise the spiritual challenge of forgiving and accepting in love a world that may not have met one's hopes and expectations. For a further discussion of spiritual issues, see Part VI.

2. *Share your own grief experiences, but don't compare them with those of the bereaved.*

If you have suffered the loss of a loved one, your insights may be very helpful to the bereaved. In sharing your bereavement remember that each loss is unique. Share the experience, but don't weigh or compare it with theirs. In our talks with bereaved persons, the well-intended phrase that most often angers is "I know (understand) exactly how you feel." The bereaved is not interested in a discourse on your suffering. They are likely, however, to be grateful for your intimate understanding of the pain of loss and may find inspiration in seeing how you have coped. For example, "When Bobby died, for months I thought my life was over. Then one morning, I saw the sun streaming through the kitchen window and I was, again, glad to be alive."

3. *Include a quotation, reading, or historic letter.*

On occasion the words of another may touch a sentiment that strikes a chord in your heart. By all means, use them! The purpose in writing a letter of condolence is to convey your sympathy as authentically and caringly as possible. If a poet's words echo your own message, it is a gift. A selection of quotations begins on page 223. Historic letters are found throughout Part III, Different Losses, Different Griefs.

It may seem surprising, but those in grief have also told us how inspiring and healing historic letters can be. Many of these historic letters nourish the spirit and have the potential to create a deeper realization of the universal nature of grief. Some of these letters touch our souls, lifting us out of unawareness and into awareness, out of pain and into gratitude. Although the letters have been written in the distant past, their expressions of sympathy may capture what you wish to convey.

SYMPATHY NOTES: THE FOUR COMPONENTS

On occasion, you may wish to express your sympathy in a short note rather than a letter. Or, you may wish to write a brief personal note on a commercial condolence card. We suggest that you consider including the following four of the seven basic components described previously. If, for the sake of time or other considerations, you wish to send a card or telegram, you may want to refer to Chapter 6, Just a Few Words.

A Sympathy Note: Example

Dear Deborah,

1. **Acknowledge the loss.**

   Our family was deeply saddened today when we heard from Bill that you had lost your mother.

2. **Express your sympathy.**

   We are all thinking of you and send our heartfelt sympathy.

3. **Note special qualities of the deceased or the bereaved, or recount a memory about the deceased.**

   In the years we lived next door, your mother was the most wonderful neighbor! She was always warm, gracious, and ready to lend a hand. We feel fortunate to have known her.

4. Close with a thoughtful word or phrase.

With affection and deepest condolences.

IF YOU'RE HAVING DIFFICULTY WRITING

When you're writing a letter of condolence or sympathy note, keep thinking of *what* you want to say, not the "proper" way to say it. Often, words don't flow easily. Too many letter-writing guides insist on form and style at the expense of the writer's personality. Remember that the most important thing is the sentiment. Ideally, a letter of condolence should be written as if you were speaking with the bereaved. If you keep focusing on what and how you are feeling, the words will usually take care of themselves. The first way of saying it that comes to your mind is often the best. It's your way; it expresses your personality.

We have given the following suggestion to many who wished to convey their sympathy, but experienced difficulty in finding the words. Before beginning, close your eyes and visualize the person to whom you are writing. Don't try to structure the image; instead, let it come forth naturally. Notice what feelings, thoughts, and memories emerge. Imagine what you would do or say if you were with the person at that moment. Open your eyes and quickly jot down any words or phrases that came to you during the visualization. Don't organize or edit at this time; let your thoughts flow even if they don't immediately make sense to you.

For example, if in your visualization you found yourself speechless, but reached out and took the bereaved's hand or offered a hug, then in your letter talk about your feeling to reach out your hand or hold the bereaved in your arms. If in your imagination you heard yourself say, "I never realized how much I loved Ben's laughter; we could use a little bit of that right about now," say it!

Now we suggest that you repeat the process in a slightly different way. This time, visualize the person who has died. Again, notice what feelings, thoughts, and memories emerge.

If you have difficulty, imagine a time when you were actually with that person. The image that comes will help stimulate your feelings. Open your eyes and write them down.

You can repeat either process a number of times before you write the actual letter. Be aware that these visualizations may stimulate your own feelings of sadness. If this occurs, allow it. It's natural. Out of these feelings come words from the heart.

Chapter 6

Just a Few Words

SYMPATHY CARDS

In letters and notes of condolence we attempt to express sentiments so often passed off as inexpressible. We want to acknowledge that each grief is unique, but at the same time we recognize that loss is universal. This paradox raises the challenge of addressing both individual circumstance and common human experience. With care, the message that we extend in a condolence letter can also be transmitted with a sympathy card.

While commercial sympathy cards may appear impersonal to some, they are a boon to many. Their sentiments vary greatly. The following samples are courtesy of American Greetings, one of the nation's foremost publishers of greeting cards. These examples range from formal messages that serve primarily to acknowledge the event and offer condolence:

> May this message serve
> as an expression of deep
> and sincere sympathy.

to personal expressions of compassion:

> If only there were something
> That friends could say or do,
> Some way they might express their thoughts
> And help to comfort you—
> And yet, perhaps just knowing
> That there are those who care

Will help, at least in some small way,
To ease the loss you bear.

to inspirational messages or biblical quotations that reassure the bereaved of God's caring presence:

God is our refuge and our strength,
a very present help in trouble.
—Psalms 46:1

In recent years, greeting card publishers have recognized interest in another format. The messages on these cards reflect an openness to spirituality separate and apart from the traditional Judeo-Christian belief in an afterlife. The following example also conveys a message of compassion when the death of a loved one has come as a release, as in after a long and painful illness.

Think of your loved one
As someone whose work is done,
Whose troubles are now past,
Entering gladly
Through that friendly door
To "Home at last."

The epigrammatist, Ashleigh Brilliant, is another whose cards reflect a new vision of loss, often expressed with poignancy and insight. For example, one of his cards reads: "People who are never completely forgotten,/Never completely die."

In a report by American Greetings, three features were most often sought by the public when selecting sympathy cards: (1) that the bereaved's sorrow is shared by others, (2) that memories are a resource to help healing over time, and (3) that there is comfort in the closeness of others. Many purchasers also seek cards that affirm their belief in an afterlife.

Why purchase a sympathy card rather than write a personal note?

- A sympathy card may be an appropriate first expression of one's sorrow. It may be sent off immediately upon hearing of the loss and followed by a letter in the next few weeks.
- The writer may know the bereaved only formally or from a distance, such that an unadorned expression of sympathy is appropriate.
- Some writers feel overwhelmed by a blank piece of paper. Here, the graphic design of the commercial sympathy card and the sentiment already expressed may prompt the sender to compose an additional personal statement or write an entire condolence letter, essentially using the card as stationery.
- The printed message on a sympathy card may be personalized by underlining or highlighting words. The deceased's name may be written in to replace expressions like "Your loved one." A handwritten message can supplement the printed text. Consider the increased impact possible when simply adding to a preprinted sentiment, "This message so beautifully puts into words what I feel in my heart."

Don't limit your communication to a sympathy card when the bereaved or the deceased is a close friend. In this case, a thoughtful letter of condolence provides a far more healing vehicle for your words of comfort.

Remember that the grief following a profound loss is rarely resolved in a matter of weeks. All too often, those in grief are overwhelmed by expressions of sympathy in the days immediately following a loss, but are left to their own devices soon afterward. Cards sent over a period of time can be a wonderful support to the bereaved.

We came across a beautiful example of "follow through" in this series of handwritten messages added to commercial cards by a condoling friend. The writer sent them over the course of several weeks to a woman whose sister had just died.

Hello Dear Friend!

How are you doing these days? Are you eating well? Sleeping? Staying at work too late? Keeping in touch with the people who care? The answers better be: Better! Yes! Yes! No! Don't forget, I care!

Dear Sharon,

Are you exercising? Eating well? Getting your rest? You'd better be!

I hope you remember how special you are—and that we've got tickets for the ballgame in two weeks.

Sharon, love,

Just me again, tapping you on the shoulder to say hi. How are you today? Hope you're feeling better. Remember—I care about you!

Dear Sharon,

How's it going? Did you have a good weekend at the beach? There isn't much to say, but I've been thinking of you. Love.

Remember that even in the most formal of circumstances, a handwritten message on a sympathy card—no matter how brief—catapults that expression of sympathy into a much more significant statement of caring.

SYMPATHY TELEGRAMS

Upon hearing the news of a death, you may wish to take any number of actions. You could choose to telephone, send flowers or a gift, visit immediately, sit down to compose a letter of condolence, or send a card or a telegram. Why a telegram? If the geographical distance is far, the appropriateness is obvious. But even if you reside nearby, a telegram can be very meaningful.

In more than a century of use, the telegram has consistently been associated with a message of significance. Its cost, speed of delivery, and need for concise wording have set it apart as a unique form of communication. A telegram can fulfill special functions at a time of bereavement.

1. It quickly communicates your wish to reach out in sympathy.
2. It permits immediate acknowledgment of the loss without what for some might be an imposing or intrusive phone call.
3. As with a letter, a telegram may be cherished and referred to over time.

For the writer, the telegram presents a somewhat different challenge than does a letter of condolence. While unusually brief, it must still communicate the writer's sympathy and concern; see the examples below. Often, sending a telegram is a first step in offering condolence, but in some cases, depending on the message and the relationship of the sender to the bereaved, the telegram may be sufficient on its own. For example, a telegram is a perfectly appropriate format for a message of condolence to the family of a famous person or public figure who is known only by reputation to the writer. A telegram may also stand on its own where the relationship of the writer to both the deceased and the bereaved family is somewhat distant. However, in general, a telegram is most appropriately followed by a letter, phone call, or personal visit.

> In this time of your deep loss we extend to you our sorrow and tender understanding.

> What a terrible shock. It is difficult to convey our deep sadness, but our thoughts and love are with you.

> Feeling very close to you and sharing your sorrow. Will call soon, once your heart has had a little rest.

Grief is a heartache that slowly heals. Your lovely daughter will be missed sadly, but she will always be in our hearts.

Our heartfelt condolences and deepest sympathies in your time of sorrow. Letter follows.

Our sympathies. May the gentle sunshine of memories be a light in this hour of darkness.

Your dear grandfather is gone from our touch, but never our hearts. The loss is more ours than his. Let us remember him through the echo of his laughter.

Please accept deepest sympathies. The healing will require courage and patience. Our prayers/love/thoughts are with you in this time of grief.

We have just learned with profound sorrow of the death of your mother and send sincere condolences. Will phone this weekend.

Our thoughts and love are with you. We have so many wonderful memories of times with your brother. He was a very precious gift to us all.

You are remembered with warmth, sympathy, and understanding in this time of sorrow.

I'm so very sorry to hear of the death of your father. Please accept my profound sympathy and my prayers. God bless you.

Thinking of you at this time and extending our heartfelt understanding and sympathy. We have lost a wonderful friend.

We are saddened by the news of Ronald's passing. Please accept our sincere sympathies. Our professional/business community has lost a valuable and respected member and we have lost a cherished friend. We will miss him deeply.

Part III

Different Losses, Different Griefs

To every thing there is a season, and a
time to every purpose under the heaven:
A time to be born, and a time to die;
A time to plant, and a time to pluck up
that which is planted;
A time to kill, and a time to heal;
A time to break down, and a time to build up;
A time to weep, and a time to laugh;
A time to mourn, and a time to dance.

—ECCLESIASTES 3:1–4

Chapter 7

A Death in the Family

UPON THE DEATH OF A PARENT

As adults, we think we understand. We recognize that, in the natural order of things, parents are likely to die before their children. As we enter maturity and our parents enter old age, we like to feel that we are, to some degree, prepared for the inevitable. In one sense it is easier to accept parental loss without the feelings of rage and bewilderment that so often accompany the death of someone in their youth. But when we love, there is never enough time.

The loss of a parent is the single most common form of bereavement in the United States. Even after Edward Myers wrote an entire book on the subject, *When Parents Die,* he questioned his own understanding of the phenomenon:

> What does a parent's death mean? Ultimately, despite my own experiences, despite my research, despite my thinking over the whole matter for years, I have to admit that I don't know. Not really; not fully. How can I grasp the fact that my parents made my life possible? How can I perceive the depth of their influence on my childhood? How can I calculate the effects of what they gave me, showed me, taught me over a period of twenty or thirty years? Until I can answer these questions, I have to doubt how deeply and broadly I understand their deaths. (p. 175)

The experience of condoling one whose parent has died touches a universal chord. While many in the world will never lose a spouse or a child, each of us is a son or daughter, and most of us will experience parental death. In the process of sharing our sympathy over the death of another's parent, there is great opportunity for an enhanced awareness and appreciation of the subtle complexities in our own parental bonds.

FOR ADULTS

1. *Regardless of a child's age and experience, one's parent is always one's parent and adult children typically feel as pained and as shaken as any others in grief.* The parent-child bond remains a part of one's identity throughout life. Fortunately, adult children have the advantage of life experience to assist them in coping with the death of their parents. However, the mind's logic and the heart's pain have little to do with each other at a time of loss. An ancient Hassidic story illustrates this poignantly:

> There once was an 85-year-old man whose 103-year-old father had just died after a joyous and productive life. In their efforts to console his deep grief, the son's friends reminded him of the long, rich, and blessed life his father had lived. "Why," they asked, "do you weep with such anguish?" The bereaved man looked up, eyes filled with tears, and said, "Though my heart aches for the absence of my father, that is not why I weep. I weep because yesterday, I was a son. Today, I am just an old man."

2. *Upon a second parent's death, many adults suddenly feel the weight of responsibility as the now oldest generation in the family.* There are no longer parents to fall back on. Moreover, a parent's death may cause anxiety as it heightens realization of one's own mortality. The presence of parents is a psychological buffer between children and death; when the buffer is gone the adult child is suddenly confronted by being the "next in line."

In addition, unexpected feelings akin to orphanhood sometimes arise. Even the mature "child" of age sixty or older may experience a loneliness and emptiness that has the quality of parental abandonment.

3. *Because deep grief in an adult child is considered by some to be unnecessary and even inappropriate, the grief process may be stifled.* Often, well-meaning friends respond to the bereaved whose parent has died by asking how the surviving parent is "holding up," thus neglecting the grief of the grown son or daughter. In addition, if this is the first parent to die, the adult child often feels a responsibility, whether innate or imposed by society, to focus support on the surviving parent. In doing so, he or she may neglect or avoid his or her own need to grieve.

4. *When death comes as a release after a parent's slow decline, as with debilitating disease, there is time for gradual adjustment to the anticipated loss.* This period provides an opportunity to resolve old conflicts, prepare material concerns, and softly say good-bye. Edwin Schneidman, in *Voices of Death,* describes the process:

> Premourning is made up of droplets of acute grief—the deep and overwhelming sense of loss and abandonment—while the loved person is still alive but obviously dying. Its psychological function would seem to be to inure the potential survivor, step by step—while there is still time—before the loved one's death, so that the event itself does not have the shocking effect of a sudden and unexpected catastrophe. (p. 147)

A slow decline may also have its own particular burdens including ongoing obligations of emotional and financial support and enormous time commitments. For the child who has been the parental caretaker, grief may be complicated by exhaustion, depression, and underlying feelings of guilt over the natural relief experienced after the death.

5. *In spite of the strain and obligation that may follow the death of the first parent, the situation can foster a positive turning point in the relationship between the child and the surviving parent.* It can strengthen bonds and deepen feelings of mutual gratitude and respect. The realization that time is precious allows old misunderstandings to fall away as the relationship is more deeply cherished.

6. *If you are condoling an adult whose parent has died and you're unclear as to the nature of their relationship, err on the side of assuming that it was a positive one.* Even if this was not the case, the loss will be deeply felt and expressions of sympathy are almost always appreciated. If the relationship was highly conflicted, keep in mind that resolution of grief may be even more complex than usual. Even though there may be an initial feeling of relief on the part of the bereaved, be aware that anger and guilt often follow.

For Adolescents

1. *Adolescence is normally a time of inner turmoil, but with the addition of a parental death, young coping mechanisms are often strained to their limits.* An adolescent may respond in any number of ways ranging from withdrawal to rebellious and antisocial behavior. The surviving parent, often immersed in his or her own grief, may be irritable, distant, inaccessible, or deeply depressed. Thus, the adolescent child may feel unsupported or abandoned. Some adolescents express the feeling, at least temporarily, that they have lost not one but two parents.

2. *In this time of upheaval, adolescents may feel awkward, fear rejection from their peers, and even experience embarrassment over a parent's death.* These emotions are normal, but often cause the adolescent to feel confused, angry, and alone. In his autobiography, *Cavett,* coauthored with Christopher Porterfield (Harcourt Brace Jovanovich, 1974), Dick Cavett vividly describes his reaction following the death of his mother from cancer when he was only ten. It seemed to him that he was the only child to whom this had ever happened. "I still can't talk about it easily. I was in fifth grade at the time, and having a dying mother was, aside from the sadness, an acute embarrassment. . . . Maudlin sympathy angered and somehow shamed me." (pp. 21–22)

For Children

1. *A child's ability to comprehend death is different at each of three broadly defined stages of development.* From ages three to five,

children often see death as a reversible separation, a temporary state that is like sleep. For many months after the death, young children may ask, "When is Daddy coming home?" Between the ages of five and nine, a child may accept the death of a person or pet but not necessarily the fact that everyone will die, including loved ones and the child herself. The child frequently views death as not due to natural causes but as a result of strife, defiance of authority, retaliation, or punishment. Concerns about death often involve personal security; the child wonders in a concrete way, "Who will cook dinner now that Mommy is gone?" By age nine or ten, most children begin to comprehend death as an inevitable experience for everyone, including themselves.

2. *When a parent dies, small children are often sadly overlooked.* The child's primary source of support is usually the surviving parent who has been traumatically affected by the death of a spouse. The child is bewildered and confused by the surviving parent's grief. Widows and widowers, usually sad, anxious, and insecure following the death of a spouse, frequently express impatience and irritation with children who simultaneously have special needs.

3. *Probably the most intolerable conviction that a child can bear is that he is not wanted.* In misguided efforts to spare children pain, adults may say, "Mommy or Daddy has gone away for a while." If the lost parent is perceived as having gone away voluntarily, feelings of rejection and abandonment often follow. The child's grief becomes a struggle against crushing walls of distress caused by anger, impaired self-esteem, and feelings of worthlessness.

4. *Many children have underlying feelings of guilt after the death of a parent.* One aspect of normal psychological growth is the occasional "secret wish" that a parent would go away forever or die. Help children understand that even if they have had this wish, they are not responsible for their parent's death.

5. *Do not tell children that "God loved Daddy so much that he took him to heaven."* This may complicate the child's grief with resentment toward a God who takes parents away.

6. *Avoid well-meaning and frequently heard statements such as "You will have to take care of your father now," or "Now you're the man in the family."* Remarks like "Be strong and take your mother's place" put an incomprehensible burden on the child. It is far more supportive to comment on the child's own positive strengths.

7. *Do not underestimate the impact of a letter that touches the heart and mind of a child beset with sadness and fear.* There is a particular need for truth, simplicity, clarity, and support. As adults who have experienced some of the trials of life we have an important responsibility to share our life's experience with children. If we are not caring and honest in our condolences, children will usually sense our guardedness and duplicity and are likely to respond by rejecting our actions.

LETTERS OF CONDOLENCE UPON THE DEATH OF A PARENT

ADULTS TO ADULTS

Dear Dwight,

I just learned of the death of your father. I'm deeply sorry. The shock was a great one even though it was expected. But he went as he would have wished—peacefully and without suffering. It is we who loved him who feel the pain. Kahlil Gibran has said, "Pain is the breaking of the shell that encloses [our] understanding." Having known your father, I understand much more deeply the simple joys of life.

Your dad was so special to me; he always seemed to have the time and patience to answer any question. Yes, I, too, loved him and I share in your grief. How I wish that sharing it could lighten the burden for you. But I also know that your own strength and courage, which have been demonstrated many times through the years, will help you meet this painful challenge.

It would be a gift for me to help you through this period. When we get together on Friday, let's begin to see what needs doing.

My thoughts and sympathy are with you.

Dear Richard,

Today I heard that you have lost your parents. The suddenness of it must have been an overwhelming blow; I just can't tell you how sorry I am. Having so recently been faced with the death of my mother, I know only too well the pain of it.

Everyone who knew your parents respected and had great affection for them. Their many good works in the community have been, and will continue to be, an inspiration to us all.

Life can be tough, but then so are we. We may feel fragile, but we're actually pretty resilient. We surprise ourselves, and others too, by picking up the pieces—moving through our bad times, facing life's challenge, and seeing the beauty of the world once again.

I'm sorry to be so far away at your time of need, but I will stop by just as soon as I return home next month. You have my deepest condolences.

Dear Wendy and Spencer,

The news of your mother's death, while not unexpected, was nevertheless a blow. The final word is so definite always. I want to express my deep sympathy, but also, I feel a quiet understanding that your beloved mother—who suffered so long—has finally found release. I can only imagine what the loss means to you and the rest of the family. You can all take great comfort from the fact that each and every one of you did everything possible—far beyond the call of duty—to make your mother's last troublesome days as easy for her as possible. She loved her family and knew that they loved her.

Dorothy's friends know how extraordinary a woman

she was, as a wife, as a mother, as a friend, and as a co-worker. She has left her mark on us and we know that we have lost a great friend whose life was a pattern to guide us and an inspiration to live by. May God comfort you and ease your pain.

My Dear Margaret,

We've just heard the sad news and hasten to offer our sympathy. Terry and I cannot tell you how shocked we were to hear of your sudden, great loss. Everyone who knew your mother loved and admired her. We can only imagine how vast your sorrow must be.

Everyone says you were a most wonderful daughter. We agree! Knowing this, let your heart be at ease.

You have our love and friendship always.

This letter was written to Clara Clemens upon the death of her father, Mark Twain, the renowned American author and humorist. The condoler was one of Twain's lifelong friends.

April 22, 1910
My dear Clara,

I found Mr. Pain's telegram when I came in late last night; and suddenly your father was set apart from all other men in a strange majesty. Death has touched his familiar image into historic grandeur.

You have lost a father. Shall I dare tell you of the desolation of an old man who has lost a friend, and finds himself alone in the great world which has now wholly perished around?

We all join in sending you our helpless love.

Yours affectionately,
W. D. Howells

The extraordinary letter of condolence that follows provides a rare glimpse of Benjamin Franklin. He wrote it to his niece upon the death of his brother, her much loved stepfather. The comfort he offers comes through his view of this life and the life that comes after.

February 23, 1756

I condole with you. We have lost a most dear and valuable relation. But it is the will of God and nature, that these mortal bodies be laid aside, when the soul is to enter into real life. This is rather an embryo state, a preparation for living.

A man is not completely born until he is dead. Why then should we grieve, that a new child is born among the immortals, a new member added to their happy society? We are spirits. That bodies should be lent us, while they can afford us pleasure, assist us in acquiring knowledge, or in doing good to our fellow creatures, is a kind and benevolent act of God. When they become unfit for these purposes, and afford us pain instead of pleasure, instead of an aid become an encumbrance, and answer none of the intentions for which they were given, it is equally kind and benevolent, that a way is provided by which we may get rid of them. Death is that way. . . .

Our friend and we were invited abroad on a party of pleasure, which is to last forever. His chair was ready first, and he is gone before us. We could not all conveniently start together; and why should you and I be grieved at this, since we are soon to follow, and know where to find him?

Adieu,
B. Franklin

Adults to Children

Dearest Tiffany,

You are very young to be so brave and I know that everyone who saw you yesterday is proud of you. Like you, I was small when my father died, so I know that sometimes it will seem lonely for you. But you have many things to comfort you. You have all the beautiful memories of the things you did together and the time you spent with him, and that is important. But more important are the things you have to look forward to.

You have your mother who loves you dearly. You have all the fun and excitement that goes along with growing up—new places to visit, all kinds of new experiences and activities. You also have a new responsibility. And that is to grow up the way your Daddy would have liked to see you grow up.

I've learned to know you and love you through the Blue Bird meetings. You are a charming, thoughtful, talented, determined girl and I feel sure that you don't need all this advice, but I want to give you any encouragement I can. Just remember that I'm here if you want to talk with someone.

With much love,

———

Dear Brian,

This morning I heard that your mom died just a few hours after the terrible car accident. You must feel awful and very sad. Our whole family also feels sad because your mother was such a wonderful person.

In the next few weeks, many things will be different. Sometimes sadness makes us feel angry, and confused. You and your sisters and brother and dad need to be extra loving to each other. As hard as it is, if there is one thing that I've learned about sadness, it's that talking about how you feel really helps.

I love you very much and I'll talk with you real soon.

TEENAGERS TO TEENAGERS

The following letter is from a teenager to a friend who lost her mother.

Dear Christine,

I was really shocked when I heard about your Mom. I couldn't believe it. Tears just started pouring out of my eyes. I have never been in your situation and I really don't know what to say except that I am thinking of you all the time. I know if it were my mother I'd want to slam the door and never face anyone again. You must be really hurting.

I can't say I knew your mom well, 'cause I didn't. But she was always friendly and really made me feel welcome whenever I came over.

Christine, I want you to know how glad I am that we're friends. I have been taking extra good notes at school, even in Buxbaum's class (he gets more boring every day). When you're feeling like it, I could come over and help you catch up. Please call if you just want to talk.

Love and tears,

This next letter is from a teenager to his cousin.

Dear Jeff,

Sorry it's taken me so long to write. I was feeling very sad. I would really like to sympathize with your sorrow. I would really like to tell you how I feel, but I can't find the words to say.

You know I always felt very close to Uncle Jesse; he was my favorite Uncle and one of my favorite people. I especially loved the sunny outlook he had and his ability to make people laugh and feel good. In going through my things I came across pictures from last summer and it's hard to believe he's really gone.

I want you to know how much I enjoyed seeing all of you last summer. We had such a super time. I always felt you and your dad had a great relationship! Uncle Jesse has often been in my thoughts even though I didn't see him that much, and he will remain in my heart.

Mom and Dad said it would be great if you could

come and visit us this Christmas. Me, too. Maybe we could take a ski lesson or just sit around the lodge—a lot of people you know will be there.

Love,

CHILD TO CHILD

The letter below is from a seven-year-old child to a friend whose father died.

Dear Tony,

I am sorry your father died. I am so sorry I want to cry. He was really a great dad. We had such a great time when he took us to the circus. I don't understand why he died.

Will you come back to school soon? I want you to come back to school and I miss playing with you at recess.

Love,
Stephen

CHILD TO ADULT

An eight-year-old child wrote to a teacher whose father had been killed in the line of duty as a firefighter.

Dear Ms. McCullough,

I'm feeling awful about what has happened to Mr. McCullough. Your father had courage, and a lot, too. And here is a poem

Roses are red, violets are blue,
I am sorry to hear that awful news,
But do not forget I am thinking
About you and your family too.

I hope you come back soon. Our substitute is okay, but not as good as you.

Your student,

UPON THE DEATH OF A SPOUSE

> To have and to hold from this day forward, for better, for worse, for richer, for poorer, in sickness and in health, to love and to cherish till death do us part.
>
> THE BOOK OF COMMON PRAYER

We acknowledge it from the start. We say, "till death do us part," but in the magic of the moment few are really prepared to hear the message. With every commitment to relationship comes the risk of loss.

Although the strength of the marital relationship varies from one marriage to another, most contain powerful bonds. For some, marriage is born out of an all-consuming and passionate love where the loved one comes to mean everything. For others, marriage grows out of friendship into deep intimacy.

Even in marriages fraught with difficulties, the grief response of the surviving spouse may be very strong. In fact, there is evidence to suggest that the survivors of troubled marriages have a more difficult adjustment during bereavement. Feelings of guilt, anger, and regret may be stronger than in the survivors of healthy relationships. Once a partner has died, there is no longer hope for resolution of problems or for strengthening the marriage. Accepting the reality of unfinished business and unresolved feelings is frequently difficult and extremely painful.

No matter what the nature of the bond between them, the death of a husband or wife is often the most profoundly disturbing and disruptive event in adult life. Spouses are typically co-managers of home and family; they are companions and sexual partners. They are co-adventurers in the journey through life. When a spouse dies, the sharing of dreams, hopes, and the years of growth together suddenly become memories and shadows.

1. *The severing of the marital bond typically catapults the survivor into psychological disorganization out of which the bereaved must redefine himself or herself as an individual.* Even when common

sense tells the bereaved that he or she was a full and happy person before the relationship, resourceful and independent, the death of a spouse often brings with it both a weakening of one's sense of self-worth and a surety that nothing will ever again be the same.

2. *For a surviving spouse, the looming burden of being solely responsible, especially if there are children, is often overwhelming.* Immersed in pain and bewilderment, it may be very difficult to respond to the needs of grieving children. Even when the surviving parent is able to tap inner resources and speak with the children about their love and their loss, the parent may be surprised by the children's ways of responding. C. S. Lewis, in *A Grief Observed,* gives us a glimpse of his experience following the death of his wife:

> I cannot talk to the children about her. The moment I try, there appears on their faces neither grief, nor love, nor fear, nor pity, but the most fatal of all nonconductors, embarrassment. They look as if I were committing an indecency. They are longing for me to stop. I felt just the same after my own mother's death when my father mentioned her. I can't blame them. It's the way boys are. (p. 8).

Children have their own limits. It is important to be open with children while encouraging questions and remaining sensitive to their capacity to understand. (Further discussion on children's grief may be found earlier in this chapter in the section "Upon the Death of a Parent.")

3. *The workplace may either be a wonderfully supportive environment for the bereaved or may reinforce suppression of grief.* Occasionally, the grieving spouse may become totally involved in work as an escape from friends, relatives, and even relationships with co-workers. Such avoidant behavior is easy for the bereaved to rationalize at the moment and may even feel constructive. While this sort of retreat can be appropriate for a time, over a prolonged period it will take its toll in depression, isolation, and other emotional problems.

4. *If a spouse has died after a terminal illness, the survivor may have begun to grieve even before the death.* Knowing ahead of time can be a blessing if it is used to begin the grieving process, but not everyone is secure enough to fully confront the reality of terminal illness in a loved one. It is important to remember that no matter how one has anticipated a death, the surviving spouse will still experience shock and disbelief when the death finally occurs.

5. *In older age, with limited material or social resources, and/or failing health, the surviving spouse may only see a deteriorating, difficult, and painful future.* Since the partnership of marriage typically serves to divide household responsibilities, the survivor may be left burdened by unfamiliar tasks. Often, after the loss of a spouse, people feel ill-equipped to assume new roles and feel unable to meet the demands of adequately sustaining themselves in a complex world. For instance, a new widow is sometimes forced to change roles sooner than she feels ready. She must learn to cope with the insecurity of possible incompetence, handle anxieties brought about by unfamiliar decision making, and perhaps adjust to a new standard of living.

6. *Beyond the fear that they may not be able to cope with the tasks of day-to-day life, those who have lost their life's partner may experience a dread of loneliness and loss of meaning.* Noted psychoanalyst, Frieda Fromm-Reichmann, has written: "People are more frightened of being lonely than of being hungry, or being deprived of sleep, or of having their sexual needs unfulfilled." For some, the enormity of facing old age alone looms like a dark cloud, obscuring the sky in every direction. It's a time when friends need to make their caring felt.

7. *Anxiety concerning social isolation and social inadequacy emerges early in bereavement.* The surviving spouse is confronted by fears, real and unreal, of a change in status. The newly bereaved may rapidly discover that they no longer have access to previously available social supports. Much of our culture is couple-oriented and widows or widowers may

present awkward social problems and embarrassing situations for even their closest friends. For some couples, the presence of a surviving spouse underscores the impermanence of their own relationship. Friends—whether out of a desire to give the bereaved grieving time or out of their own discomfort—may avoid the bereaved. Happily, there are others who will offer compassion, support, and a new closeness.

8. *This tumultuous time also carries with it the potential for dramatic and constructive change.* The belief system that governed their life was shattered. After a time, the bereaved may begin to think, feel, and behave in ways that reflect a positive new perception of themselves and the world, although they may be floundering for direction well into their second year. As Stephen Schuchter, M.D., and Sidney Zisook, M.D., write in the May 1986 *Psychiatric Annals,*

> Over time, these beliefs will be replaced by new ones reflecting the finiteness and fragility of life and limits of control. As a result, the bereaved often become more appreciative of daily living, more patient and accepting, more giving. They may develop new careers or change them, enjoy themselves with more gusto, or find new outlets for creativity. (p. 34)

Each bereaved spouse must heal in his or her own way. Each needs to give himself or herself permission to do this and to reestablish a personal identity. However beautiful the past, at some point the bereaved spouse must be willing to accept the challenge of a world redefined.

LETTERS OF CONDOLENCE UPON THE DEATH OF A SPOUSE

Dear Ted,

It was with a very sad heart that I heard the news just the other day of the passing of your sweet wife and my dear friend, Ellie. Words fail in telling you just how badly I feel. I'm sure you are aware that I was very fond of Ellie, both as a friend and as a co-worker on our many projects.

Ellie was a delightful person in so many ways. I always anticipated with pleasure our working together. She was creative, hard-working, and reliable. A real team player. She was funny, too, and that is a priceless commodity when you're feeling the stress of a deadline.

Although you and I met only rarely, I feel I know you from all the little stories Ellie used to share over coffee breaks. She never had anything but happy things to say about her life with you and the kids. Last spring she brought in pictures from your trip to Vermont and she just lit up as she described your tobogganing with the children. She loved you all very much.

My children and I are smoking a couple of hams and will bring one over when it's done just right. In the meantime, my sincere condolences to you and the whole family on your great loss.

———

Dear Margaret,

This morning, when Susan told me the news about your darling Jim, I sat down and wept. While his loss was not unexpected, I still felt a wave of disbelief. I am so sorry.

Jim was such a gifted man: in his profession, in his wood carving, in his family and friends, and in his readiness to share his thoughts and feelings.

The last time we spoke, just before the reunion, I asked if he felt his illness was affecting the way he looked at life. He didn't brush me off or avoid the issue in any way—that wasn't Jim's style—instead he paused, reflected for a moment, and said, "It seems the world is topsy turvy; so many of the little things I used to feel were important have just fallen away while many of the small moments I once took for granted are incredibly precious." You came up at just that moment with a cool drink and a warm smile. As you walked away Jim grinned and said, "See that? That's one of those precious moments."

I can only imagine how deeply you feel this loss, Margaret, but you can take solace in all the loving ways you cared for Jim—not just in his last illness, but through a long and happy marriage. He could always count on your support as he tackled new challenges and he respected your opinion immensely. You two were partners in a way it seems few married people are these days. Now it will be your challenge to take the same strength of character and good sense that you shared with your husband and direct it toward your own rich life. Your friends may never "match" you in the way Jim did, but they love you and respect you and are there to help you in any way they can.

Count on me, will you? I'll drop by in the next couple of days to see if there's anything I can do to help. . . . I'll call first. In the meanwhile, take very good care of yourself.

Dear Alex,

For the past day, my thoughts have been of nothing but you and the beautiful Julia. I don't know if there's anything that can be said to soften the pain of your grief just now, but my love, my unqualified friendship, and my prayers are with you.

Julia was such a vibrant spirit. Her exuberance made life around her a constant adventure. You joined her on that adventure with all your heart, whether sailing through the islands or sitting silently by a mountain stream. There was a sense among many who knew you that you each embraced fully the unknowable mystery that is life. I guess the mystery just gets deeper.

I'm reminded of a short piece by Henry Van Dyke. It's called "A Parable of Immortality":

> I am standing upon the seashore. A ship at my side spreads her white sails to the morning breeze and starts for the blue ocean. She is an object of beauty and strength, and I stand and watch until at last she

hangs like a speck of white cloud just where the sea and sky come down to mingle with each other. Then someone at my side says, "There she goes!"

Gone where? Gone from my sight . . . that is all. She is just as large in mast and hull and spar as she was when she left my side and just as able to bear her load of living freight to the place of destination. Her diminished size is in me, not in her. And just at the moment when someone at my side says, "There she goes!" there are other eyes watching her coming and other voices ready to take up the glad shout, "Here she comes!"

So, Alex, may the winds of life blow gently around you at this difficult time. I want to help in any way I'm able. I'll call Thursday.

In trust and friendship,

The following touching letter by a father to his bereaved daughter is an example of a significant deviation from usual form. Yet, its love, honesty, and humor go right to the heart.

My Daughter Lisa,

Ole Frankie is off on another cruise. That carpenter, plumber, champion bread maker, and oh yes, musician. He could beat a drum! For ten years we were friends; the feeling was mutual between us. My mother had an expression in her tongue—she "kvelled" when her guests at her table ate with gusto, and I always did too, to watch Frankie down a hamburger.

I feel I've had a pretty good bite out of life, but ole Frankie had lived more in his nearly sixty years than I have in my nearly eighty-five. He not only took a bite out of life; he chewed it up.

Yes, I'll miss that old Devil, but somewhere, sometime, out there we will meet and you know what we will talk about—some gal's rear view!

Love you,
Dad

Dear Mrs. Melton,

Yesterday I read in the paper about Mr. Melton's death. Please accept my deepest condolences.

Everyone has special people in their life who stretch their horizons and are positive influences. Mr. Melton was one of those people for me. As a teacher, he was always supportive and made me feel that I could face any challenge. I will not forget him.

I hope you take some comfort in knowing how many others there are like me who were profoundly touched by your husband's work.

Sigmund Freud's daughter, Sophie, died suddenly in January 1920 from the virulent influenza that was sweeping across Europe. Freud's three sons had come home from World War I safely, so the irony of the young woman's death was particularly felt by the psychoanalyst. He wrote this touching letter to Sophie's husband.

Dear Max,

It seems to me that I have never written anything more superfluous than this. You know how deeply we feel for you. We know how badly you yourself must feel. But I won't try to comfort you, just as you cannot comfort us. Perhaps you feel that I do not know what it means to lose a beloved wife and the mother of one's children, because I have not had to endure the experience. You are right, but I know how unbearable it must be to survive such an experience. I need not tell you that this misfortune does not change anything in my feelings toward you and that you remain our son as long as you wish to do so. It goes without saying that this follows from our earlier relationship, so why do I write to you? I think it is only because we are separated, and that in these miserable times we cannot meet, and thus I cannot say to you the things which I say to mother and to brothers and sisters. It is a senseless brutal act of fate which has taken our Sophie from us, something that one cannot wrack one's brain about, a blow under which we have to bow our heads, poor helpless human beings that we are. I think she was happy as long as she was with you, despite the difficult times of your short seven-year marriage, and her happiness was due to you. . . .

When President Woodrow Wilson's wife died during World War I, his ambassador to Great Britain, Walter H. Page, responded with this letter.

Bachelor's Farm
Ockham, Surrey
Sunday, August 9, 1914
My dear Wilson:

There is nothing that even your oldest and nearest friends can say—words fail in the face of a bereavement like this. But I can't resist the impulse to write how deeply I feel for you.

You would be touched if I could tell you the number of good men and women who every hour of the day and night have expressed to me the grief with which they heard the sad news—men and women who never saw you, from King down to the English messenger in our embassy. . . .

But, my dear friend, it hits us hardest who have known you longest and love you most and who wish for you now all possible strength, in this sad, sad hour of the world when, more than any other man in the world, you are most needed—all possible strength to you. If the deep sympathy of all your friends, known and unknown to you, can help to support you and to keep your high spirit and courage up, you have it in most abundant measure.

Mrs. Page and I grieve with you and hope for you to the utmost.

Yours with affectionate sympathy,

Upon the death of Robert Louis Stevenson, author of *Kidnapped* and *Treasure Island,* Henry James, devoted friend of the Stevensons and noted author himself, wrote this letter to Stevenson's widow, Fanny. What a remarkable letter this is.

December 26, 1894
My dear Fanny Stevenson.

What can I say to you that will not seem cruelly irrelevant and vain? We have been sitting in darkness for nearly a fortnight, but what is *our* darkness to the extinction of your magnificent light? . . . All this time my thoughts have hovered round you all, around *you* in particular, with a tenderness of which I could have wished you might have, afar-off, the divination. You are such a visible picture of desolation that I need to remind myself that courage and patience and fortitude are also abundantly with you. You are all much to each other, I am sure, and the devotion that Louis inspires—and of which all the air about you is surely full—must also be much to you. Yet as I write the word, indeed, I am almost ashamed of it—as if anything *could* be "much" in the presence of such an abysmal void. To have lived in the light of the splendid life, that beautiful, bountiful being—only to see it, from one moment to the other, converted into a fable as strange and romantic as one of his own, a thing that *has* been and has ended, is an anguish into which no one can enter with you fully and of which no one can drain the cup *for* you.

You are nearest to the pain, because you were nearest to the joy and the pride. But if it is anything to you to know that no woman was ever more felt *with,* and that your personal grief is the intensely personal grief of innumerable hearts and devotions—know it well, my dear Fanny Stevenson, for during all these days there has been friendship for you in the very air.

For myself, how shall I tell you how much poorer and shabbier the whole world seems and how one of the closest and strongest reasons for going on, for trying and doing, for planning and dreaming of the future, has dropped in an instant out of life. I was haunted indeed with a sense that I should never again see him—but it was one of the best things in life that he was *there,* or that one had him, at any rate, one heard him and felt him and awaited him and counted him into everything one most loved and lived for.

He lighted up a whole side of the globe and was in himself a whole province of one's imagination. We are smaller fry and meaner people without him.

I feel as if there were a certain indelicacy in saying it to you, save that I know there is nothing narrow or selfish in your sense of loss—for *himself*. However, for his happy name and his great visible good fortune, it strikes one as another matter, I mean that I feel him to have been as happy in his death (struck down that way, as by the gods, in a clear, glorious hour) as he had been in his fame, and, with all the sad allowances, in his rich, full life.

He had the *best* of it—the thick of the fray, the loudest of the music, the freshest and finest of himself. It isn't as if there had been no full achievement and no supreme thing. It was all intense, all gallant, all exquisite from the first, and the recognition, the experience, the fruition had something dramatically complete in them. He has gone in time not to be old—early enough to be so generously young and late enough to have drunk deep of the cup. There have been—I think—for men of letters few deaths more romantically right. Forgive me, I beg you, what may sound cold-blooded in such words—and as if I imagined there could be anything for you, "right" in the rupture of such an affection and the loss of such a presence. I have in my mind, in that view, only the rounded career and the consecrated work. When I think of your own situation I fall into a mere confusion of pity and wonder—with the sole sense of your being as brave a spirit as *he* was (all of whose bravery you endlessly shared) to hold on by. Of what solutions and decisions you see before you we shall hear in time—meanwhile please believe that I am most affectionately with you. . . .

. . . More than I can say, I hope your first prostration

and bewilderment are over, and that you are seeing your way and feeling all sorts of encompassing and supporting arms—all sorts of outstretched hands of friendship. Don't, my dear Fanny Stevenson, be unconscious of *mine,* and believe me more than ever faithfully yours.

Henry James

George Eliot, British novelist (born Mary Ann Evans) and author of *Silas Marner, Middlemarch,* and *The Mill on the Floss,* wrote this letter of condolence to Mrs. Charles Bray. Charles's friendship and philosophy of social responsibility had a profound impact on the life of Eliot.

The Priory, March 18, 1865

I believe you are one of the few who can understand that in certain crises direct expression of sympathy is the least possible to those who most feel sympathy. If I could have been with you in bodily presence, I should have sat silent, thinking silence a sign of feeling that speech, trying to be wise, must always spoil.

The truest things one can say about Death are the oldest, simplest things that everybody knows by rote, but that no one knows really till death has come very close. And when that inward teaching is going on, it seems pitiful presumption for those who are outside to be saying anything. There is no such thing as consolation when we have made the lot of another our own. I don't know whether you strongly share, as I do, the old belief that made men say the gods loved those who died young. It seems to me truer than ever, now life has become more complex, and more and more difficult problems have to be worked out. . . .

But I will not write of judgments and opinions. What I want my letter to tell you is that I love you truly, gratefully, unchangeably.

UPON THE DEATH OF A CHILD

I kept saying to myself, "Wake up, wake up. This is just a bad dream. There is no way my friend could have been killed. This is all a dream."

But this was reality, and I think reality really hit me when the funeral began. What hurt me most was seeing his father crying at his own son's grave.

—HIGH SCHOOL SOPHOMORE
UPON THE DEATH OF A SEVENTEEN-YEAR-OLD FRIEND

When children die the world seems unnatural, unfair, and unthinkably cruel. No matter what the age of a child, whether unborn baby, infant, young person, adolescent, or adult, the death of a child fragments our life-cycle expectations. Parents expect to die before their children; it seems the "right" order of things. Whether the death of a child occurs in stillbirth, after a lingering illness, or suddenly, as from an accident—even if there are other children—an empty space remains. Life goes on, but it takes a new form. Sigmund Freud, the father of psychoanalysis, described this poignantly:

> Although we know that after . . . a loss the acute state of mourning will subside, we also know we shall remain inconsolable and will never find a substitute. No matter what may fill the gap, even if it is filled completely, it nevertheless remains something else. And actually this is how it should be. It is the only way of perpetuating that love which we do not want to relinquish.

For parents, children exist not merely as children. They are our creation and the part of us we expect to endure beyond our lifetime. A child, in the deepest sense, is a piece of oneself. So the death of a child is not only felt as the absence of a loved individual but as the amputation of an essential part of ourselves, something that can never be replaced once it is gone.

When a child dies, parents are not only bereft of their child's presence but also of all the promises and dreams that might have been. Thus, the grief after a child's death is frequently one of the longest and most difficult types to resolve. Shakespeare captured the desperation and longing that may shift the mind and cause it to replace the child with the suffering of grief itself:

> King Philip: You are as fond of grief as of your child.
> Constance: Grief fills the room up of my absent child,
> Lies in his bed, walks up and down with me.
> Puts on his pretty looks, repeats his words,
> . . . Then, have I reason to be fond of grief?
> —*King John,* Act III, sc. 4

Perhaps more than in any other grieving, after the death of a child, parents ask, "Why did God do this to me?" This question reverberates with an unceasing and hollow echo. In the depths of their grief they cannot fathom that a benevolent God might allow such a misfortune to happen. Even among the great religious teachers, the death of a child may test one's grasp of the mysterious ways of life.

In the tradition of the Tibetans is the story of Marpa, a great spiritual master of a thousand years ago. Marpa taught his disciples that all was illusion, yet one day—soon after the death of Marpa's son—one of his disciples found the master weeping at the river's edge. The disciple was shocked: "You have taught us that all is illusion, yet you grieve over the death of your child. I do not understand."

Marpa turned to his disciple, saying, "It is true. All is illusion, and the death of a child is the greatest illusion of all."

Those who follow the teachings of this spiritual master speak of his vision of the paradoxical nature of life. There are, according to Marpa, two planes of existence. Simply put, in the first plane, all is illusion, mysterious and wondrous. In the second, the plane in which we live our daily lives, it is inevitable that we experience all the joys and sorrows of life.

The search for consolation after the death of a child has the power to elevate one's faith in the unending and unfathomable mystery of existence. In his poem, "On an Infant Dying as Soon as Born," Charles Lamb wrote:

Riddle of destiny, who can show
What thy short visit meant, or know
What thy errand here below?

When writing or speaking with parents, the struggle to condole, to say something to touch their anguish, is as old as history. Try. Some will readily hear your message. In *The Oxford Book of Death* Friedrich Rückert is quoted from his *Songs on the Death of Children:*

You must not shut the night inside you,
But endlessly in light the dark immerse.
A tiny lamp has gone out in my tent—
I bless the flame that warms the universe. (p. 109)

For Adults

1. *The manner in which a child has died is likely to affect the form of grief that follows and influence the way in which we condole.* The grief for a child lost through miscarriage, stillbirth, or in the neonatal period must not be underestimated. In miscarriages, the grief of parents is often poorly recognized by others. Those who do recognize the loss typically consider the parents' grief to be less important than it would be with a physically known child. This is often not so. The grief may be intense, complicated by confusion about the cause, self-doubt, and feelings of guilt. Mothers seem to bear the brunt of these emotions. When the baby was long wanted, sadness may turn to despair. If you are unclear about what to do, respond with sensitivity as you would to the death of any child.

Each year in the United States one stillbirth occurs in approximately every hundred deliveries. The aftermath is overwhelming. Plans for celebration are transformed into plans for a funeral. Joy becomes pain, embarrassment, and guilt. Gratitude toward God may become anger and resentment.

When a stillbirth occurs, the family is often stunned and plagued by questions tinged with self-recrimination, such as "Could we have caused this?" "Could we have prevented it?" In well-meaning efforts to spare the parents suffering, hospital personnel may all too quickly remove the child's body. As in miscarriage, friends with the best intentions may say, "It's better this way; you really never knew the child." Society's guidelines are unclear as to how we should provide comfort at such times. Funeral services may be abbreviated or may not be held at all. There sometimes seems to be an unwitting conspiracy to make the death a nonevent, an invisible tragedy.

For parents, however, the tragedy is hardly invisible. They often experience crushing despair and grief. Even before birth, the baby's personality was felt; the child may already have been given a name. There were hopes, dreams, ambitions, and prayers for the baby long before it was born. Attachment and bonding had already begun. The reality of such a death is hardly a nonevent; it is the death of a child deeply loved.

Sudden infant death syndrome (SIDS) takes the life of more than 10,000 infants in the United States annually. Its exact cause is unknown. In SIDS, an apparently healthy baby is typically found dead in its crib; thus the term "crib death." There are no previous signs of illness or sounds of distress and there can be no blame. However, parents who have lost a child to this syndrome are often torn apart by guilt and self-recrimination. Their life had been totally immersed in the wonder and responsibility of the new baby and strong bonds were formed. Grief is intense and many survivors find solace and guidance through SIDS support groups. Condoling friends need to make their understanding, caring, and presence repeatedly felt over what may be a long grief period.

When a child dies after an extended illness, parents may first have had to cope with the child's suffering. Long-term emotional upheavals can have a devastating impact on individual integrity and family organization. Yet with anticipation of the coming death, the grief has already begun. When some of the pain of loss has occurred before the death, the shock that follows may be less acute and the grief more accessible. Still, the problems to be faced are enormous. As with many treasures of inner value, we are not always fully conscious of the vital and cherished place a child has in our life. The mind is often unable to assess the full impact of a major loss until it is upon us.

When the death of a child is the result of an accident, many of the same issues arise that we recognize in the grief following any sudden death. Some of these points are addressed in the section Upon Death by Suicide, Violence, or Accident in Chapter 8.

2. *Although guilt and anger are present in most bereavement situations, they are likely to be especially pronounced following the death of a child.* Guilt, in particular, can be emotionally incapacitating. Parents frequently feel guilty just for being alive, sometimes wishing that they, not their child, had died.

3. *The crisis brought about by a child's death is a cataclysmic event that challenges every marriage.* For some couples, although the death of a child casts them into a shadowed valley, the understanding between them may yield a tenderness and mutual support that rises above the clumsiness of words and the agony of loss. However, it is not uncommon for marriages to falter under the immense strain imposed by a child's death.

Marital discord is frequent and the number of couples who divorce after a child dies is far higher than in the general population. Often, husbands and wives will experience the death of their child in different ways. Not only may their experiences be different but the manner in which they grieve may be different. Parents need to give each other permission to grieve in their own unique ways. Yet, it is not typically these differences that create the marital problems. More often, they are the result of difficulties in communication, especially at a time when each is caught in private anguish. Partners find it difficult to tap those inner resources usually available to support and assist the healing of the other in times of crisis. In the mind's search for a rational answer, husbands and wives often blame each other.

4. *The depth and intensity of a father's grief is often camouflaged in our culture.* Fathers frequently assume outward expressions of strength in an effort to help maintain family equilibrium. As a result, well-meaning friends may focus their condoling attentions on the bereaved mother. Although it often manifests differently, the grief of fathers must not be overlooked or underestimated.

5. *In offering your sympathy remember not only the parents and siblings but the grandparents, whose mourning often goes unnoticed.* Of course, when a child dies grandparents bear their own grief for the loss of the beloved grandchild, but there is more. Their pain is compounded by having to watch the suffering of their own adult child. In many ways, it is a double tragedy for grandparents. For this reason, and for the unfortunately infrequent acknowledgment, your expression of condolence to grandparents will be doubly appreciated.

6. *For some families, belief in an afterlife or reincarnation often comes to the foreground as they try to make sense of the child's death.* How are parents to find solace when, in the words of Plautus, "He whom the gods love dies young"? While in Nepal, Dr. Zunin participated in meditation sessions at Kopan Monastery. Following one session, Lama Thubten Yeshe invited questions from those present. In the stillness of the gathering was a feeling of trust that opened the way for intimate inquiries. At one point a young, sad-looking woman spoke softly and asked the Lama to help her understand the recent death of her four-year-old boy. The Lama looked up with a knowing and gentle smile as he explained:

> Such a high soul—a beautiful being chose to be born through your womb for this incarnation on earth. This time he had so little work he needed to accomplish. This time his work on earth was a reward and a blessing. This time his soul was to be set free early. Rejoice in his blessings. Rejoice in your gift. Judge not the joy of his soul by the length of his life on earth or you will miss the fragrance of the beyond. Spread your love for your child to all beings and your suf-

fering will melt away like a dew drop in the morning sun and your understanding will blossom like a lotus in springtime.

For Children

1. *When young friends or siblings die, surviving children suffer their own sadness and their capacity for grief often goes unrecognized.* The expression of children's grief is different from that of adults. Frequently, they don't want to share their feelings, in part because they are fearful that doing so will make parents and other loved ones sad. Children need to be reassured that talking about sad feelings is a good thing and it will help them and all who love them to feel better.

Parents, distraught and exhausted, sometimes find it difficult to pick up signals that children use in the place of verbalizing their fears and sadness. During this time, teachers and friends may more easily notice changes in a grieving child's behavior. Nonverbal manifestations of childhood grief include shifts in behavior such as withdrawal or rebelliousness, disruptions in eating or sleeping habits, or physical complaints such as headaches or frequent stomachaches. Subconscious fears about their own death sometimes become evident in nightmares.

2. *Children may be easily overlooked when a family is in mourning.* Overcome with their own grief and personal needs after the death of a child, parents often become, for a time, insensitive and inaccessible to their other children. Children may interpret their parents' preoccupation as rejection and frequently experience confusion and resentment over the feeling that they have been shunted aside during a sibling's terminal illness and/or death. One way in which to support grieving children is to mention them by name in letters of condolence to the family. Better still, write a note or send a small gift directly to the children. When visiting, talk with them. You need not necessarily talk about the death or their grief; just include them in your conversation and activities.

3. *Witnessing their parents' grief or the grief of other adults is often frightening to children.* Children are worried by what they perceive to be their parents' instability, suffering, and the resultant failure to care for them in the usual manner. Grieving children need frequent reassurances of love and that their world is still on solid ground.

4. *Children, more than adults, typically experience a greater sense of guilt and fear during bereavement.* Young children especially associate death with punishment. It's as if the deceased, having committed some wrongdoing, was "sent away." Following this childhood logic, grieving youngsters may feel that their own death will soon come as punishment for misdeeds or bad thoughts.

5. *Communicating the truth to children when a death in the family occurs—both facts and feelings—is extremely important.* When we avoid discussing death with children under the guise of protecting them, we need to realize that this neglect is often due to our own discomfort with death. Not to discuss with children our thoughts, our feelings, our beliefs, and our fears about death is a disservice to them and often a misjudgment of their capacity to understand. Even the saddest day can be endured by children when the experience and suffering are shared. Encouraging their expressions of grief and allowing them to participate in whatever funeral ceremonies may occur are critical in the meaningful sharing of family grief. Further information on the grief of a child can be found in the section Upon the Death of a Parent.

LETTERS OF CONDOLENCE UPON THE DEATH OF A CHILD

Dear Ginny and Paul,

There are no words to adequately express our shock and grief. We just heard the sad news that you lost the baby today. What a terrible blow to have the anticipation of a joyous birth turn into such an occasion for sorrow. We know it won't change anything, but we want you to know that all of us here at the office are grieving right along with you. Our hearts are filled with sadness.

Although your love for the baby will be with you always, we hope and pray that time will quickly soften the anguish. Don't worry about work; we're all covering for you (although yours are mighty big shoes to fill). Margaret, Julia, and I will be by this weekend and hope we can help out with any chores that need doing.

With love and sympathy to you both in this great loss.

Dear Lauren and Edgar,

Keiko and I want to express our profound sorrow on the loss of your beloved infant son.

Although his journey on Earth was brief and he never bathed in the sun, from his conception he was bathed in your love and surrounded by your very being. He is part of you as surely as you are part of him.

We are reminded of a short poem by the sixteenth-century Japanese poet, Teitoku Matsunaga:

> The morning glory blooms but for an hour
> and yet it differs not at heart
> From the giant pine
> that lives for a thousand years.

We're sending you our love and a special hello to Billy from his pal Rusty who says he's bringing all his Leggos on Saturday when we come by for a visit.

This touching letter is one of many in a useful little booklet, "How to Write Letters for All Occasions," by Abigail Van Buren of "Dear Abby" fame.

Dear Sally and Fred,

What is there to say? You know how Mel and I feel about the loss of little Angela. Perhaps this bit of philosophy that we enclose will help you in your sorrow. It was given to my sister when she lost her only daughter, aged 8. She said it was the most comforting of all the messages she received:

> Once there was a beautiful procession taking place in heaven. It was a long, long, line of lovely little children marching through the pearly gates. Each carried a lighted candle. Their smiling little faces shone as their candles reflected their glow. One little child sat alone in a corner, sad and forlorn. When one of the happy marching children asked why she was not marching with the rest of the happy children, she replied, "I would like to, but every time I light my candle my mother puts it out with her tears."

Our love,
Lucy and Mel

My Dear Friend Arleta,

Mother just telephoned and told me your nephew died yesterday. I was terribly saddened to hear the news. An accident such as this must be an awful shock.

I know from your stories and from your wonderful photos what a bright and spirited presence Gregory was in your life. Through your sadness I know you will remember his winning smile.

If there is any little way that I can be of service, I would be honored. Please extend my heartfelt sympathy to Greg's parents.

Dear Sasha and Leon,

We read in this morning's paper of the death of your talented son, Benjamin. We share with many the shock and sorrow of this tragic news; and our hearts go out in sympathy to you and his wife and family.

There are times after long illness when death seems to be "for the best." Some even look upon it almost as a blessing rather than a great sorrow. But for the heart, the loss of a loved one—especially a child—is never a blessing.

> How hard this painful year has been for all of you. But we have been profoundly touched by your courage, your caring, and your unswerving devotion. You have not only been of tremendous assistance to Benjamin but you have been an inspiration to us all.
>
> We remember fondly the reception for his first one-man photography show years ago; Benjamin was beaming! We still recall with a smile his words as he watched the crowd: "I can't believe so many people have come to see what I do for fun."
>
> Our hearts are filled with sympathy for you, for the long year of suffering, and for your sorrow now that your son is gone.

The timelessness of grief and consolation echo through the centuries in this letter from a husband to his wife. It was written in the first century by Plutarch, the Greek philosopher and historian. Far from home, Plutarch had just received word of the death of his two-year-old daughter. Both the child and her mother were named Timoxena. The language of the translation may seem awkward at first, but the sentiment is profound.

> Dearest Timoxena,
>
> . . . I conceive and measure in mine own heart this losse, according to the nature and greatnesse thereof, and so I esteem of it accordingly; but if I should finde that you took it impatiently, this would be much more grievous unto me and wound my heart more, than the calamity it selfe that causeth it; and yet am I not begotten and born either of an Oak or a Rock; whereof you can bare me good witnesse, knowing that we both together have reared many of our children at home in house, even with our own hands; and how I loved this girle most tenderly, both for that you were very desirous (after four sons, one after another in a row) to bear a daughter, as also for that in regard of that fancy, I took occasion to give her your name; now besides that natural fatherly affection which commonly men have toward little babes, there was one particular property

that gave an edge thereto, and caused me to love her above the rest; and that was a special grace that she had, to make joy and pleasure, and the same without any mixture at all of curstnesse or forwardnesse, and nothing given to whining and complaint; for she was of a wonderful kind and gentle nature, loving she was again to those that loved her, and marvellous desirous to gratifie and pleasure others . . . as if upon a singular courtesie and humanity she could find in her heart to communicate and distribute from her own table, even the best things she had, among them that did her any pleasure.

. . . I see no reason (sweet wife) why these lovely qualities and such like, wherein we took contentment and joy in her lifetime, should disquiet and trouble us now, after her death, when we either think or make relation of them: and I fear againe, lest by our dolour and grief we abandon and put clean away all the remembrance thereof . . . for naturally we seek to flee all that troubleth and offendeth us. We ought, therefore, not so to demean ourselves that as whiles she lived, we had nothing in the world more sweet to embrace, more pleasant to see, or delectable to hear than our daughter; so the cogitation of her may still abide and live with us all our life time, having by many degrees our joy multiplyed more than our heavinesse augmented. . . .

[Remember] . . . our soul is incorruptible and immortal . . . it returneth thither again, and re-entreth a second time (after many generations) into the body. . . .

Chapter 8

Special Situations

UPON DEATH BY SUICIDE, VIOLENCE, OR ACCIDENT

What if there are no good-byes? What if death comes suddenly? The characteristic common to all sudden deaths is the loss of an opportunity for the bereaved to bid their friend or loved one good-bye. Whether by suicide, homicide, manslaughter, or accident, this crucial issue complicates and compounds grief. Bereavement is painful no matter what the cause, but bereavement following the sudden death of a close friend or loved family member is a uniquely personal and interpersonal tragedy. It is also a reminder of the fragility of human life.

If you are fortunate enough to know when your loved one is dying you have the possibility of taking an active role in the parting process. This may be experienced as a burden or a precious opportunity. In either case, there are many choices to be made. You may visit or pull away. You may choose to talk openly about fears and concerns, express your love, complete unfinished business, pray or meditate together, or join in making future decisions. However, in the case of sudden death, all these choices are torn away.

Suicide

1. *The suicide of a friend or loved one brings with it a legacy of confusion, guilt, blame, hostility, stigma, and feelings of rejection.* Those left behind may also experience an unsettling relief over a troubled person's suicide. The recent extraordinary

rise in the number of suicides among teenagers and the elderly has captured the concern of society. There is an increasing segment of the population that sees suicide as a viable alternative to the final phase of terminal illness. Generally, however, death by self-destruction is typically more difficult to accept and understand than other deaths.

2. *Feelings of rejection following a suicide are almost universal.* Here, we refer to the self-destructive act of a physically healthy person, not the suicide of a terminally ill person who has made a personal decision to abbreviate a life of pain or accelerated deterioration. Although the death of a loved one by any cause may leave even the most stable among us with feelings of abandonment, these feelings are heightened subsequent to suicide.

3. *Blame and guilt often go hand in hand following a suicide.* Those in grief may unconsciously look for a scapegoat—a person, object, or situation on which they can blame the death. The surviving spouse, parents, siblings, or friends may blame each other for not seeing the signs of impending suicide or for not meeting the needs of the deceased. If blame is focused inward, the result is guilt. The bereaved often feel a sense of responsibility for the death, berating themselves for what they believe they did not see or do. Inner feelings of rage over being abandoned and socially embarrassed further intensify survivors' grief.

4. *Social stigma compounds the problems of loved ones following a suicide.* Suicide has a way of exposing private matters to public questioning and speculation; for the general population, it remains a socially unacceptable death. Anxiety over the judgments of others can be terribly painful. Whether from shame or anticipation of blame, those close to the deceased are often reluctant to fully discuss the event. This reluctance to express themselves interferes with the natural grieving process. Your willingness to acknowledge that suicide was the cause of death, while remaining authentically caring or loving, is appropriate and can be extremely impor-

tant in opening the way for acceptance, conversation, and the healing of grief.

5. *The stress of social stigma combined with the potent mechanism of denial may prompt the bereaved to unconsciously create acceptable stories or myths to explain the death.* This is particularly likely following probable but not proven suicides. It serves several purposes: relieving guilt, diminishing social embarrassment, and eliminating potential social stigmatization. If survivors do not accept the possibility that the deceased took his or her own life, they can avoid facing the notion that the person who committed suicide consciously abandoned them.

6. *There is no more suitable time to discuss the concept of forgiveness than in the wake of a suicide.* There are two aspects to consider. The first is forgiving the deceased for having taken his or her life. While the concept of forgiving one who has died may sound strange, this kind of forgiveness is primarily an internal process, much like prayer. As with prayer, the answer is heard within. This means having room in one's heart to see another's choices, whatever they've been, and to accept them.

The second aspect involves forgiving oneself in the presence of guilt for not having done more. It is critical to the healing process. If bereaved individuals experience self-blame, they must gradually let go of feeling responsible, angry, and guilty for the acts of a loved one. Without this important step, full healing cannot occur. Condoling friends who are accepting and persistent in their caring contacts are invaluable.

7. *Some terminally ill and elderly feel that suicide is preferable to what may be the physical deterioration, isolation, pain, and loneliness of their final days.* For them, suicide is a viable option, the result of a well-thought-out, rational decision. This circumstance is on the rise with the advent of AIDS (see later in this chapter) and increasing concerns over quality of life in light of technological advances in medicine. If you, as a condoling friend, have difficulty accepting suicide as a conscious choice, every attempt should be made to refrain from expressing such a judgment in the first throes of grief. At a later date you

may wish to discuss your feelings with the bereaved, but let your initial words of condolence, whether in writing or in person, be nonjudgmental. Simply support the healing process.

VIOLENCE

1. *Violent deaths are primarily caused by accident, natural disaster, manslaughter, or homicide.* Precisely because these deaths are so shattering to the fabric of life as we know it, the bereaved often receive less, rather than more, support from loved ones and friends. This is largely due to understandable insecurities about what to write, say, or do.

2. *Senseless! is a term that reverberates with a hollow echo in the mind of the bereaved following a violent death.* This feeling that the death was meaningless evokes profound and unsettling emotions. Your acknowledging the senselessness of the act will be far more supportive than any attempt to rationalize.

3. *In deaths due to homicide or manslaughter, rage and blame naturally follow.* Even those who are ordinarily mild-mannered may find themselves considering violent revenge. Recognizing in themselves the capacity to even fantasize in such a way can create powerful sensations of fear and guilt. The fear is of losing control; the guilt is in harboring such emotions.

If the death was by murder or manslaughter and the perpetrator is alive, forgiveness may seem impossible. It is the greatest challenge for the bereaved. Aspects of forgiveness are discussed earlier in this chapter.

4. *The public nature of many violent deaths adds another complication to the grieving process.* Following such an event, the bereaved may be involved with legal procedures including investigators, trials, attorneys, the media, and added expenses. These things may prolong the duration of the grieving process. Offers of help from trusted friends are particularly important in the face of so complex an upheaval, one that is both internal and external.

5. *If the body is mutilated, grief is greatly compounded.* Whether one is an atheist or believes in an eternal spirit, the soul in heaven or reincarnation, the violation of the physical body still causes anguish. Reconstructing memories of the physical image of the deceased is an integral part of the healing process of grief. Over time, the bereaved typically create a composite mental picture of their loved one. A mutilated body at death, whether it has been seen by the bereaved or not, evokes fantasies and feelings that interfere with the process whose goal is to mentally re-create the loved one as a healthy being.

6. *Guilt is likely to be devastating in situations where the bereaved was involved in the accidental death of a loved one. If there is even a question of negligence on the part of the bereaved, the guilt may be incapacitating.* This is a time when condoling may seem nearly impossible, and yet a time when it is most needed. Rather than focusing on the circumstances of the death, let your words speak of your awareness of the terrible emotional pain the bereaved is going through.

7. *Fearful preoccupation often follows in the wake of a violent death. Such deaths may provoke in the bereaved a preoccupation with their own death or that of another loved one who is dying.* These fears, often unspoken, can trigger somatic disorders, anxiety, and changes in life-style. Sorting out the realistic from the irrational fears takes time and requires support and patience from loved ones. Professional assistance and support groups are often very helpful. Additional information on bereavement resources is found in Chapter 17, Grief Therapy and Support Groups.

LETTERS OF CONDOLENCE UPON DEATH BY SUICIDE, VIOLENCE, OR ACCIDENT

This letter was written to a husband after his wife's suicide:

> Dear Maurice,
>
> How could this have happened! What terrible news for you to have received.

Your friends all know of your years of love and tireless devotion to your wife. The agony of her deep depressions seemed unrelenting, no matter what was done during the course of the long illness to help her come to grips with herself. I know it may be difficult, but please don't blame or reproach yourself. You did so very much for Pat. All your friends are filled with sympathy, admiration, and affection for you at this time.

It's true that no one else can ever really share the sadness and agony that you're experiencing. Yet I want you to know how very much I care. I also feel the pain of this happening.

I'll be calling in the next few days. Maybe I can help with some things around the house. Give it some thought; I really want to!

The letter below is to a man following the suicide of his brother. The brother had struggled with chronic mental illness beginning in his final year at college.

Dear John,

This morning I heard about Tim's suicide. I ache for you. Ten years ago I felt your pain when, in the midst of youthful promise, schizophrenia came over Tim like a dark cloud. Your hopes and his dreams were shattered. I can only imagine how difficult this illness was for Tim, but I know how agonizing it has been for everyone who loved him to witness the unshakable hold of the disease despite the love and support of your family and all the efforts of modern medicine.

Tim's death reminded me of a letter I came across during research for my thesis. Charlotte Bronte wrote this with a certain delicate frankness following her brother's untimely death—thought by some to have been suicide:

> I do not weep from a sense of bereavement—there is no prop withdrawn, no consolation torn away, no dear companion lost—but for the wreck of talent, the ruin of promise, the untimely dreary extinction of

> what might have been a burning and a shining light. My brother was a year my junior. I had aspirations and ambitions for him once, long ago—they have perished mournfully. . . . I trust time will allay these feelings.

These words may not be conventional expressions of comfort, but they speak an important truth for me. Perhaps, for you too. Build on resolve, not on regret. I'm thinking of you and I'll be in touch early next week.

This letter was written to parents after the accidental death of their son at the hands of a drunk driver:

> Dear Mr. and Mrs. Hildebrand,
>
> Danny's death came as a tragic shock to us. We only heard about the accident yesterday. Our hearts go out to you. The death of a child never seems to make sense, but at the hands of a drunk driver it's all even more bewildering. We offer you our profound and heartfelt sympathy in your sorrow.
>
> We will always remember Danny as we last saw him. It was at the park and he had driven over just to say hello and to let us know that he was home from college. He said, with that casual shrug of his wide shoulders, he'd had his best semester ever!
>
> Danny was always full of life and optimism. Even in his passing he will remain an inspiration in our hearts as you were an inspiration to him. The best and the brightest.
>
> We are sending a contribution in Danny's memory to Mothers Against Drunk Driving.
>
> Again, our prayers and sincere condolences.

Following is a letter to the parents of a young woman who was murdered:

> Dear Dr. and Mrs. Rodriguez,
>
> It is with feelings of profound distress that we heard the very sad news of your daughter's death under such

tragic circumstances. Her untimely passing is a most severe and grievous loss. There is no sense to it on Earth; we can only look to Jesus, Our Lord.

> Cast your burden on the Lord, and He will sustain you.
>
> —Psalms 55:22

We want to express our own deep sadness. Perhaps no words that we say will ease the pain, anguish, or emptiness that you feel in your hearts, but we want you to know that we will remember your daughter as a graceful, loving, and open-hearted girl who brightened the neighborhood with her smile.

It may seem impossible now, but while nothing will ever bring Eileen back, we hope that one day you will find a source of comfort in beautiful memories of the years of joy God gave you together.

May God bless you and keep you.

UPON DEATH BY AIDS

AIDS, the late-twentieth-century epidemic, demands an increased understanding and sensitivity toward the grief of those who have lost loved ones to this tragic disease. It's true that the face of the disease is rapidly changing and that treatments already in place give us cause for hope. But there is no denying that, in an extraordinary and public way, the specter of AIDS has exposed us to countless manifestations of bereavement.

Since 1981, AIDS has burst out of obscurity to threaten the world with crippling individual, social, and economic burdens. Initially, many responded to the crisis with the denial characteristic of early grief. Others wanted to dismiss it as a nightmare from which medicine would swiftly awaken us. Some saw the disease as a scourge visited upon those who had sinned against a "moral" life. Theories abounded, but whatever the psychological response, this complex and ever-changing virus continues to destroy the immune systems of its victims, leaving them powerless against many infections.

Newsweek magazine's lead article of August 10, 1987, featured the AIDS epidemic. The story included an album of photos of many who had already died of the disease that typically has affected those in their prime:

> Each face in the album stands for a life cut short too soon; each represents a death in the American family. . . . Our habit is optimism; we are unaccustomed to an epidemic that resists the magic of our medicine, and we have too often held ourselves apart from its sufferers.

Our response to AIDS helps defines us as a society as we explore new approaches to the problems of social stigma, human rights, and the psychological trauma of death at an early age. At the same time, AIDS offers each of us a rare opportunity to test the depths of our own sensitivity and compassion, to rise above old prejudices and respond to loss out of our common humanity.

1. *AIDS is not simply a new disease; it is often associated with behavior that has been enmeshed in ancient and strongly held taboos.* Its first victims were largely homosexual men and it has since been identified as being transmitted primarily through sexual means (hetero- or homo-) or by the sharing of needles by drug abusers. This association has catapulted it into a realm altogether different from other incurable diseases. For many, the majority of AIDS victims have made unacceptable life-style choices. Whether homosexuals, sexually promiscuous, or drug abusers, the majority of its victims are considered by many to be morally deficient. The enlightened scientific age notwithstanding, their illness is seen by some as punishment for "evil" practices. Consequently, their status and persona are devalued.

2. *Transmission of the disease to so-called "innocent" victims by transfusion of infected blood has complicated our response.* Among

these victims are children born to AIDS-infected mothers, hemophiliacs, and others who received transfusions before a method for blood screening was in place. For these victims, the stigma associated with alleged "asocial" behavior seems to have been contracted with the virus. However the disease was acquired, *all* those with AIDS are innocent victims, and upon their death *all* their loved ones grieve.

3. *The social stigma associated with transmission of the disease has overwhelming psychological effects not only for the victims of AIDS but for their caregivers and loved ones.* Even after the death, the bereaved may experience social stigma. Friends and relations who under other circumstances might fully condole may instead extend only cursory sympathy to those whose lives have been tragically touched by AIDS. Fortunately, this is not always the case. Sometimes, the response to the bereaved is broad-based and inspiring.

4. *Another unique aspect in considering condolence upon death by AIDS is that the bereaved whom you wish to console may also be a victim of the disease.* Along with feelings of guilt and blame, the bereaved in this circumstance will naturally experience fear of his or her own impending death. Surviving AIDS victims may be grieving for themselves as well as for their lost partners. In addition, the self-reproach often expressed by AIDS patients is not commonly experienced by victims of other terminal conditions. This is a time when friends, more than ever, need to take a step forward. Withdrawal and depression are a frequent response both to AIDS and to grief and, however difficult, phone calls, visits, and a supportive letter of condolence can have profound and life-affirming effects.

LETTERS OF CONDOLENCE UPON DEATH BY AIDS

Dear Allen,

The news of Eric's death just reached me and I'm feeling it like a physical blow. Perhaps this isn't the time to write; my heart aches terribly. But if not now, when?

Who knows what to make of Eric's life? It's not for us to judge.

What he was in reality God only knows. That he was a man of grace is sure. That he was gifted and caring we know. That he was deeply touched by a love for his religion was strongly felt by all among us who loved him. Even when *we* were raging and ready to damn whatever being it was that had condemned him to die so wretchedly, so young, Eric was at peace with his Maker.

Maybe that's the lesson: God is the giver of grace and light. He makes allowance for those choices and situations and occurrences that cause us to travel through life on one road or another. The rest of the world? Who knows? There are probably thousands of folks who thought they were going straight to heaven, but who've been given tickets in the other direction. And then there are the Erics of this world who've been misunderstood, even reviled, and who we *know* in our hearts are tapping on those pearly gates, yea, even as we smile at our remembrances of them.

Funny, I'm feeling better having written this. And I'd meant to console you. I guess it's the work of all of us who cared for Eric to console and support and cherish one another. To fight the bitterness that sneaks around. To feel the ache and learn from it. To fill with his glowing smile the empty space in front of us. To remember. Yes, that's the work. Let's remember Eric.

I'll be over on Thursday to help you go through his things. Thanks for asking.

Dear Steve,

Wanted to let you know how sorry I was to hear about Kevin's death. Somehow I felt I had already done the grieving and was fully "prepared" until I heard the news. You think it's going to get easier each time but it doesn't.

I remember our last hilarious conversation. It keeps coming back and I hear Kevin's wonderful laughter. See you Saturday at the memorial service.

Take good care of yourself.

Dear Beth and Rick,

The sad but expected word of Joe's death just made its way to Santa Cruz. What a light has gone out for your son's many friends. Memories of him flood over me like the waves he loved to paint so much at Big Sur.

Sometime back I clipped an article from the *S. F. Examiner.* I pulled it out again when I heard the news. You will see right away why it makes me think of Joe.

> Each of us is an artist, a practitioner of the fine art of living. We're commissioned by fate to attempt one masterpiece—a life. Like most commissions, this one has a due date . . . literally, a deadline. We usually don't know when our deadline is until almost the last minute, and then we're confronted with a sudden choice: Do we start painting with ferocious urgency, or do we throw down the brushes in despair, saying it's too late to start now?

Joe neither raced ahead with "ferocious urgency" nor threw his brushes down. He was never afraid to ask himself the tough questions: What do I want to do with my life? Why not begin now? Even when confronted with his diagnosis, he forged on in his life and his art with renewed courage and passion.

Often, when we spoke on the phone, he talked of your continued love and support. It meant so much to him. He knew it had never been easy. He loved you both very much.

Thank you for inviting me to the memorial service next week. I'll be up for a few days and hope you can make time for lunch by the Bay. I'll call before then. Thinking of you with love.

Dear Daniel,

This afternoon following Sylvia's funeral, I was moved to put some of my thoughts on paper. I've been meaning to write this past week, but somehow what I wanted to say only came clear today.

Sylvia was a woman who touched the lives of many people. She was a most unusual woman: a fine attorney, a highly respected member of the community, a devoted mother, and a loving wife. She was also a staunch and uncompromising Yankees fan (who was so gracious that she even occasionally allowed Mets boosters into the house).

I remember your telling me of Bob's words when he first learned his mother was seriously ill as a result of the tainted blood with which she was transfused during her surgery several years before. He said, "It doesn't matter what the disease is called; she is very sick and she needs to know that we love her." Bob's sensitivity and understanding was a message for all of us and a reflection of the love he felt for you and his mom.

Daniel, you nursed Sylvia through a long and impossible illness. Not only did you have to deal with a dying wife but you faced daily the social and personal stigma attached to AIDS. You were able to do this with extraordinary patience, simple forgiveness, a sense of faith and hope, and the sound judgment I have seen in you so many times over the years.

As I said at the service, it was a tender and moving hour for us all. Just to confirm, I'll be over on Saturday to take you and Bob to synagogue. Much love till then.

UPON THE DEATH OF A MEMBER OF THE MILITARY

Flag-draped coffins, row upon row of white crosses at Arlington, the speeches on Veterans Day, taps played over the Tomb of the Unknown Soldier—a nation's image of military death. The military creates not only personal crises during war but also during peacetime. Whether in the trenches, an accident at sea, fighting in the streets of Panama City, or in the Persian Gulf, our military personnel sometimes die. To more clearly understand the nature of these situations, one must recognize that there are many levels and forms of commitment to the military.

Although each family is unique, military families can generally be divided into three groups based on level of commitment. The first are those for whom the military is a career inspired by dedication to its life-style and underlying philosophy. The second group are those who have become involved in the military through a personal decision to fulfill a short-term duty. This group is often associated with ambivalence and the level of commitment varies considerably from individual to individual. The final group falls somewhere between the two. These are families who do not typically embrace the military as a career, but whose short-term involvement is wholehearted. The emotional and social adjustment of each group not only to military life but to military death is influenced accordingly.

The principles we are discussing are equally applicable to men and women, and women are assuming an increasingly active role in the armed forces. It's not any easier for men to watch their wives and daughters go to war than it is for women to see their husbands and sons enter military conflict. Our focus here, however, is on the death of military men and the grief experience of their committed military families.

1. *Unlike most civilian wives, many military wives have been separated from their husbands and have been functioning independently for weeks or months prior to their husband's death.* If there have been multiple enforced separations during the marriage, as often happens in military service, "mini-grief" reactions may have occurred. Grief at widowhood may be mitigated by these separations that sometimes act as a sort of progressive immunization.

2. *Women who have married military men, especially in a time of war, clearly understand that their marriages have particular risks.* They are highly aware of the possibility that their husbands may be killed. Although this is sometimes discounted, the glaring reality hammers at the rigid wall of denial. A twenty-seven-year-old military widow shared the following experience:

That he might die? Oh yes, yes, we kind of bantered it back and forth—we had always discussed the possibility of death, always from the time we met. It was always sort of there with us. I don't know why. I suppose a great number of people do that, but we used to kid about it, you know—it was always there, but in your mind you put it off for fifty or sixty years when you think you won't care so much or something. I don't know. We had discussed it and then we discussed it again on Rest and Recreation a little bit more realistically. My husband told me things he wanted for the children, and he wanted the children to understand why he had to go and that he would, of course, rather have been with them.

During Dr. Zunin's work with military widows in group programs called Operation Second Life, it was significant that women who were able to discuss with their husbands the possibility of death prior to the men's departure generally dealt more effectively with their bereavement and made a more rapid adjustment.

3. *Widows and families of career military men rarely exude bitterness about the situation that cost the lives of husbands or sons.* They generally hold strong convictions that their men died in defense of their country and in defense of their own values of right and wrong. They want their children to believe that, too.

4. *Military widows take pride in standing on their own and living with the same courage, values, and convictions for which their husbands died.* Like all widows, military widows are lonely; they find adjustment difficult and at times slow and painful. However, as a group, they have a unique source of inspiration and rarely choose to retreat or give up. They also tend to be more reticent to ask for sympathy than many bereaved.

5. *Sometimes, the desire to carry on with strength, coupled with the necessity of maintaining the family, presents a temporary barrier to the first release of grief.* Alfred Lord Tennyson captures this experience in his moving poem "I Live for Thee":

Home they brought her warrior dead;
She nor swoon'd nor utter'd cry.
All her maidens, watching, said,
She must weep or she will die.
Then they praised him, soft and low,
Call'd him worthy to be loved,
Truest friend and noblest foe;
Yet she neither spoke nor moved.
Stole a maiden from her place,
Lightly to the warrior stept,
Took the face-cloth from the face;
Yet she neither moved nor wept.
Rose a nurse of ninety years,
Set his child upon her knee—
Like summer temptest came her tears—
"Sweet my child, I live for thee."

6. *For many women, the support of the military umbrella and association with other military widows is an additional and welcome comfort. Others choose a totally new direction in their life to help inspire a positive self-image and the birth of a "second life."* One of the military widows in Dr. Zunin's grief groups, the mother of three, wrote the following moving account reflecting on her first year of grief:

> When my husband was killed in Vietnam last year, it was the second time he had served there. We knew there was a chance of his being hurt or killed, and worried often, but he told us over and over that he knew how to take care of himself and would be back, and after so many times he had us almost convinced. The shock of being told of his sudden death by the casualty officer and chaplain is too great to express with words. It has taken me a whole year to accept his death; even now sometimes I feel like he is still out there somewhere and will be back sometime.
>
> The children now mention him more often than in the previous months. They remember things he used to do or say, and there is less sadness in their voices when they talk about him. I know, though, they still hurt and—now and then—especially if they happen to see

some news on TV about our servicemen, there is a grave look in their eyes and a twitch of their mouths which makes me think they are trying to hold back the tears. At times such as these, I suddenly put aside my own grief and turn into a clown. I say or do something silly, or tell them of something special we may do in the near future, and soon a trace of a smile appears on their faces.

> To the world he was just one,
> to us he was the whole world.

These are the words which have been engraved, at my request, on my husband's grave, and truly express how we felt for him.

LETTERS OF CONDOLENCE UPON THE DEATH OF A MEMBER OF THE MILITARY

The following letter is to a military wife from one of her husband's friends:

> Dear Janet,
>
> I have delayed in writing to you because I wanted to be sure you had been properly notified of the circumstances of Hank's death. There are few words I am capable of sending which will be of solace to you in your loss, but I want to try.
>
> In as much as I have lost many close friends in this war, I believed that nothing would come as a shock to me; however, I must admit I now sense the loss of a friend as never before. Hank's death has left a vacancy in the ranks which will never be filled in the minds of those who served with him and knew the type of individual he was. Hank's devotion to his Family, Country, and to the Marine Corps served us all as an inspiration. His personal courage, humility, straightforward manner and respect for his fellow man earned him an uncommon number of personal friends in the officer ranks of the Marine Corps and unqualified respect and

admiration from the enlisted Marines who served under him. I don't want to sound like I have climbed on a soap box, but only wanted to tell you that your loss is shared by many more than you may realize.

I heard of Hank's misfortune only minutes after it occurred and can assure you that he knew little or no pain or suffering.

Sally told me that you've displayed the type of personal courage Hank would have expected and that you face your future with confidence. One legacy that Hank has left you is an inexhaustible collection of devoted friends. I'll be in touch with you soon and hope there is something I can do to be of some assistance. I want you to understand this offer remains open to you as long as you should desire to exercise it.

My prayers and thoughts have been with you. We are all richer for having known Hank and many of us will never forget him or his family. May God be with you and your girls.

With deepest sympathy and regards,

This letter is to the parents of a young soldier killed in action:

Dear Mr. and Mrs. Fife,

Thanks for making yesterday's phone call much easier. You were right; it was not an easy one to make and I must admit that I picked up the telephone several times before I actually placed the call. Thank you, too, for asking me to participate in your son's funeral. I consider it a privilege to do that for Marty.

Both Debbie and I are very grateful and proud to know that you have the faith and strength to sustain yourself and others through this difficult period. I know that Marty would be even more proud of you.

I hope it is comforting to you to know that Marty died doing what he believed to be right. He understood and accepted the risks involved. While some men protest and tear down and debase, Marty died trying to preserve and protect and improve. It is men like Marty who provide a bright and steady light in a world that is sometimes very dark. If God wills that such men should live only twenty-five years instead of the allotted eighty or so, then it is our loss, not theirs.

When we were in Edinburgh last summer, Debbie and I visited the Scottish National War Memorial. There's an inscription there that I copied down in my journal. I now think of Marty every time I read it.

> The whole earth is the tomb of heroic men, and their story is not graven only on stone over their clay, but abides everywhere without visible symbol woven into the stuff of other men's lives.

I personally admired Marty as much as anyone I have known, and his death is a great loss to his friends, the country, and of course, to your family.

We are thinking of you. I'll be talking with you again soon.

This letter is to the brother of a Navy man killed in a training accident:

Dear Phil,

I have you much in my mind these past few days since I heard the tragic news of Greg's death.

Greg loved the Navy and serving his country. That he died in a terrible training accident may seem senseless to some. I don't feel that way. Greg's dedication was to service and excellence; he knew and accepted the risks.

He will always be an inspiration in my life and I am proud to have known your brother. I'm having a copy made of a photograph I took of Greg last year. It makes me smile and I hope it does the same for you. I'll bring it by next week.

With deepest sympathy,

Steve

This unique letter is from one military widow to another:

Dear Penny,

I'm sure you've gotten many letters from friends all saying the same thing. They all confirm what you're hoping is just something you thought up and really isn't so. Please know that with each of these letters, an understanding heart goes out to you and the children and Frank's family and yours.

I really liked Frank a lot. He just wasn't the run-of-the-mill man you meet. He had so much sincerity. I know John felt the same way just by the way they talked at a party. I remember when Frank was wearing blue jeans and John kidded him about it and I knew John wished he could wear them and look that good.

I wish we could have gotten together a few more times before we left. . . . But when John finally got his orders I was so sick inside, I just couldn't sleep or even think straight. It was particularly hard for me to say good-bye to him because, from the beginning, I knew I would never see John again. And I just let him go. I felt so helpless. Everyday I just waited for word that it was over. Of course, the news that he was wounded came when I never expected it and in a way I never thought possible. He was wounded so badly and he lived so long—8 days. I never loved a man so much in so many ways as I did John. Yet, in spite of the fact that I will never see him again, I am able to continue living very much the way I have in the past.

I think the intense pride I had in John helped me through those awful three weeks. I know how proud you must be of Frank. He was so brave. I wish we were a little closer, like across the street, but maybe we can write to each other occasionally. I sincerely hope that at any time you should come to the East Coast, you will call me.

Please take care of yourselves. John Jr. is doing very well and I thank God that He gave this little boy to me and that John was able to enjoy a little bit of proud fatherhood. I could write forever. Please keep in touch. You, Frank, and your family are in my prayers.

Sir Walter Raleigh, Scottish author and lecturer, wrote this letter to Lady Desborough upon the death of her two sons during World War I:

Oxford, August 5, 1915

I know the ordinary consolations; they do not seem to me to be quite real. But there is something quite real and consoling, if human nature could take it without ceasing to be human; we cannot work it out, that's all. But we couldn't do without Julian's life and Billy's. They are not gone, we breathe them, they are the temper of the British Army at its best. It would not matter even if they were not remembered, they passed on the flame undimmed.

The great things seem cold, but they are there all the time, and Julian and Billy believed in them, and had splendid lives. Anyhow, they have made life the little thing it is. Because of them, I am ready to say "Take it" more easily than before. What must it be for the people they fought alongside of? . . .

I go limping along. . . . And I am glad to have met and known such soldiers.

This letter was written by the German philosopher, Oswald Spengler, to his sister. Her husband, Fritz Kornhardt, had been killed in France during World War I.

Munich, April 4, 1918

Aunt Matilda has told me the sad news. At this moment I cannot write at length. Like so many others you have been made to pay the heaviest sacrifice for our country, and I feel indeed that it hits you harder than many, for Fritz and you, who have had an unusually happy life together, should not have been torn apart in so brutal a manner. I sorrow for you from the bottom of my heart, but I believe that the thought will help you over these hard days that Fritz, in respect to you, and to his profession, so also as a soldier has done his duty to the uttermost with selflessness and even self sacrifice, and that this last and greatest sacrifice will not have been made in vain.

If I can help you in any way or carry out any wish you may have, do let me know. I should be delighted if I could do you any service either now or in the future.

And keep up your courage, dear Hilde, for your own sake and for the child's. Try to find in the irrevocable a source of comfort, the remembrance of the fine and heroic, and for the future of your child look for a continuation of life which does not entirely belong to the past.

When you find time, please write to me if it is only a couple of lines. Let me assure you again that Fritz's death affects me deeply and that I am deeply sorry for you.

Elected officials typically send condolence notes to the families of military personnel killed in the performance of their duty. The following example was sent from the office of Ronald Reagan, then governor of California.

July 26, 1968

Dear:_______

It is nearly impossible to find the words to say to the wife of one who has been killed in war, because war is so senseless and the violent death of any of our men for any reason seems so meaningless.

I can only say that it is my prayer that your husband, along with those who have fought in all our wars, did not fight in vain.

Our country was built on the precept that freedom is sacred. Many Americans have fought and died for that precept, and as long as there is tyranny in the world, Americans will be called on to oppose it.

Please accept my deepest sympathy for your loss. God be with you.

Sincerely,
Ronald Reagan
Governor

Chapter 9

Professional Issues

PHYSICIANS AND OTHER HEALTH-CARE PROFESSIONALS

Nothing in our physical life is as certain or as final as its end. Confronting the inevitability of death is part of the practice of medicine and the art and science of the healing professions.

The role of a health-care professional, in its most succinct definition, is to ease suffering. It may be accomplished in many ways. For example, a condolence letter from a primary health-care professional often has a particularly special meaning when sent to loved ones following the death of a patient. Yet, although it is not rare, it is indeed infrequent that such a letter is sent. Spoken words of comfort is the usual course of action and that is why a written letter from a physician or other primary health-care worker conveys a powerfully enhanced message of caring and concern.

Following the loss of a patient, health-care professionals typically feel that they have done all that they can. At this point, they often find themselves in a peculiar situation; the healers need to shift their orientation. While the family and loved ones of the deceased may not actually be under their care, it is with these survivors that a healing must now begin. Almost as a final gift to the deceased patient, the health-care professional can help these bereaved express their feelings, accept their new reality, and feel reassured that others care and will assist if their help is needed or wanted. An important step in promoting the healing process may be taken with a thoughtful and sensitive phone call, personal contact, or letter of condolence.

1. *In the case of a lengthy illness, noting the courage of the deceased can be particularly significant, especially if the patient accepted the challenge of coping with suffering while remaining open, loving, and aware.* Coming to terms with the end of life and knowingly preparing to part from loved ones requires great courage.

2. *Briefly note special reasons for caring about this particular patient.* With care to avoid the violation of patient confidence, anecdotes and memories can enhance your message of sympathy. If you are writing, remember that the impact of your communication is greatly diminished if it has a form-letter quality.

3. *Allow your humanity, kindness, gentleness, and sensitivity to come through in your letter.* As a health-care professional you strive for harmony between your professional detachment and your very basic human feelings of compassion. This is the time to lean toward the latter.

4. *Positive reminders promote the healing process. Acknowledge the support, caring, and love of the family toward the deceased.* They will appreciate being reminded of their responsiveness to the special needs of the patient and their willingness to face realistically issues and decisions that are often difficult. Anything said to ease possible feelings of guilt is particularly relevant when coming from a health-care professional.

5. *If appropriate, express your appreciation to the loved ones for their cooperation, understanding, and assistance to you in caring for the deceased.*

6. *Anger is a part of grief.* During prolonged illness, loved ones typically form bonds of trust with those who have been primary caregivers. However, when death occurs, survivors may direct their anger and frustration at these same profes-

sionals. This is a natural outpouring of grief that must be dealt with sensitively and professionally.

7. *A letter of condolence is not the time to offer specific medical advice.* The letter will have its greatest impact if it stands as a focused message of sympathy. Advice, if given at all, should be limited. For example, encourage the bereaved to express inner feelings and thoughts and to be compassionate and caring with themselves.

LETTERS OF CONDOLENCE FROM HEALTH-CARE PROFESSIONALS

Following is a letter from an oncologist to the adult children of a cancer patient:

> Dear Derrick and Shirley:
>
> I want to express my sincerest sympathy to you on the death of your mother, Greta. We were all sensitive to your mom's wishes for her final days and they were accomplished as she wanted them to be, peacefully at home, thanks in large part to your assistance.
>
> As you know, I had grown quite fond of your mother over the years that she was my patient here, and I am pleased to have had the opportunity to serve as her personal physician. I feel that she benefited from both standard and research approaches to treatment. All too often we eventually fail in our efforts, underscoring the importance of continuing and expanding our efforts in cancer research. Your mother was always eager to try whatever the next research option was and, in fact, was still asking such questions little more than a month ago.
>
> If you should have any questions, or if there is any way I can help you, please don't hesitate to contact me.
>
> With sincerest sympathy,

A nurse wrote this letter to the widow of a patient:

Dear Mrs. Jackson,

I just learned that the inevitable happened last night. Even though it was clear that the end was imminent, the loss remains just as painful.

As one of the nurses caring for your husband during this period and seeing you almost daily, I have had the greatest respect and appreciation for your compassion through this very difficult time. My heart goes out to you. He was blessed to have had you so near.

With respect and affection,

This letter to bereaved parents was written by a pediatric surgeon who cared for their son during his brief two-year life. Stephen had been born with multiple severe congenital physical deformities.

Dear Friends,

So it has happened. That wonderfully gallant, vibrant being known to all of us as Stephen Rowe has passed into another realm of existence. Shall we not expect this beautiful being to face these new vistas with the same determination, the same vibrancy that we noted in him while he was among us. And who will stand up and tell us that Stephen Rowe is dead? Are we the same since he walked into our lives? Whatever life he has touched, is that life not changed in some manner forever? So it has been two years. Shall we make a judgment that it was not enough, that it was too short? What criterion shall we apply to his life as a yardstick to decide what is a good life and what isn't?

For my office staff and me there is only what we feel in the depths of our being. We have been profoundly affected and changed at a very basic level by the glorious energy present in Stephen. As if he reflected, in some way, that there are no criteria to judge a person's worth by simple societal guidelines. He crushed, forever, simple words, simple explanations, simple judgments, when you came in contact with him at a personal level. Here it is for the whole world to see, and to see in all its glory, that to know someone is to love them.

Our best wishes to all the family.

Most sincerely,

This letter was written by a group of physicians to the wife of a colleague who died. It was sent under the signature of the chief of medical staff:

Dear Nina and family,

We of the Valley General Hospital Medical Staff want to reiterate our deep sadness at the loss of Roy, our cherished colleague and friend. As the days melt into each other, we find that we miss him in so many ways. His great affection for the hospital, its patients, and its staff, was daily apparent in all his many activities. His responsiveness, his appreciation of life, his willingness to take the extra step whenever and wherever needed all endeared him to us.

Roy's love of learning, high standards of quality care, and sincere belief in unselfish service affected everyone privileged to work with him. In his last months at the hospital, he accepted an additional administrative challenge. His clarity, guidance, and positive attitude served all of us well in a turbulent time. Through it all, he maintained the Oslerian "equanimity" that all physicians aspire to and few achieve. He was truly in that class of men "above the common herd."

Your own courage and graciousness at so difficult a time was felt by all present at the memorial service. The obvious affection and closeness of your family must have been a great joy to Roy as it must continue to be a source of strength to you now.

We want you to know that if there is any way we can be of assistance to you we would be grateful for the opportunity to do so. I'll give you a call in a week or so.

Thornton Wilder said, "The highest tribute to the dead is not grief, but gratitude." We offer you our affectionate sympathy, many beautiful memories of a wonderful man, and our gratitude for sharing Roy with us.

Sincerely,

THE CLERGY

The theologian and philosopher, Paul Tillich, defined religion as "the ultimate concern." Whatever one's religious orientation, our concern for spiritual issues often reaches its peak when we are confronted by profound loss. Those swept into the maelstrom of grief frequently find themselves turning to their religious faith. Part VI is devoted to a discussion of spiritual matters and bereavement.

When disaster strikes there is an innate need to explain it. Such times raise unanswerable questions while the mind is desperately searching for the anchor of rational answers. Viennese psychiatrist, Viktor Frankl, experienced this realization as a survivor of the Nazi concentration camps. He wrote that human suffering is most tolerable when it is felt to be explicable—to have purpose—to have a higher meaning. The "search for meaning," Frankl concluded, is "the primary force in life."

When faith and religious beliefs are in harmony within us, religion is a love affair: a love affair with our fellow human beings, with existence, and with God. When the question of "Why Me?" arises following loss, it represents a questioning of these belief systems. One's love affair with existence cannot survive in the face of doubt; it can exist only with trust. But doubt is the usual condition, at least for a time, following the death of a loved one.

At times of loss, clergy are frequently sought out for comfort, reassurance, and assistance. Initially, of course, a minister, priest, rabbi, or other spiritual leader may officiate at the funeral or memorial service. But the greater challenge for the clergy is often to help the bereaved draw upon hidden or fragmented spiritual resources, to strengthen hope and courage, and to recall the bereaved to their sense of personal wholeness. Support in this area comes from other religious sources as well. Members of the congregation call on the bereaved. In conversations, letters, and sympathy cards, many people offer not only their sympathy but their prayers. God, prayer, and confrontation with religious beliefs clearly become more evident in the life of the bereaved.

In our research on condolence we have consulted with numerous religious leaders. Frequently they espouse a practice of only personal condolence calls to bereaved individuals. "I rarely write," said one minister. "I encourage my parishioners to, but feel that my work is best done when I sit and talk quietly with the bereaved."

While it's true that these personal visits can be of immense value to mourners, especially when they continue over a period of months, our experience has confirmed the additional powerful impact of letters of condolence from the clergy. Over and over we are told by the bereaved how precious and reaffirming such letters have been. A condolence letter from the bereaved's religious leader may be the most meaningful and cherished letter that they receive.

1. *The bereaved often look for a member of the clergy to serve as a spiritual guide to light their way through a time of suffering and anguish.* It can be very comforting, whether during a personal visit or in a letter, to have reassurances that you will continue to be available for them.

2. *Allow the expression of doubt and the questioning of faith that is so often a part of the natural grief response.* It will be particularly reassuring to the bereaved to hear from their religious leader that such feelings are normal and temporary.

3. *Few people are able to sustain themselves during intense grief with the belief that "It is God's will," or that "God has an ultimate design for each of us."* Although not impossible, it is unusual for a bereaved individual in the early stages of grief to find inner peace, equanimity, and acceptance through an openness to the mystery of all things and trust in the ways of existence.

Those in grief, especially following an early or violent death, often find the fabric of their religious beliefs frayed at the edges or even shot through with holes. The previous "garment" of beliefs may be discarded. On the other hand, with the gradual resolution of grief, a new spiritual fabric is often woven—using threads from the old—and this new spiritual cloth may be richer and deeper than the one that came before. With a series of visits, phone contacts, or a condolence letter, a revered religious leader can be a powerful influence.

4. *You may be a religious leader, interpreting God's word, giving meaning and comfort, but you are also a sensitive human being who knows the bereaved or knew the deceased in a personal way.* The bereaved is likely to deeply appreciate expressions of your personal concern and sensitivity.

5. *The greatest challenge for the religious leader is to help the grieving person find meaning, purpose, and even opportunity in grief.* This realization may come with time, but early in grief the bereaved is likely to be put off or even angered by suggestions that their suffering carries with it the opportunity for spiritual growth and greater closeness to God.

LETTERS OF CONDOLENCE FROM THE CLERGY

Dear Donna,

My sincere condolences to you and your children on your husband's death. I just heard the news from Reverend Alston.

I assure you of my prayers and remembrances this Sunday. In the freshness of your pain, I wish for you the strength to walk each day in God's light.

You have been tested before and have met the challenge with devotion and grace. Another time has come. It may feel that your heart is breaking, but remember that "He healeth the broken in heart."

May your beloved Nick rest in peace. I will phone in the next few days to see when I might visit. God bless you and the children.

Dear Rachel, Harry, and Arthur,

After presiding over today's funeral service I was so moved that I wanted to tell you again in writing what an honor it was to have known your father. What a wonderful man, such a lover of life! We heard many beautiful and heartwarming stories this morning from his friends and family, remembering Charles' unceasing optimism, but on the drive home I recalled still another—something he read to me when I visited a few weeks ago. He had just finished the book *Why Me?* by Rabbi Pesach Krauss and had been deeply touched by the message of the last few lines, so I copied them down.

> There is constant renewal of the good in life. This awareness I call faith. Windows of hope are always there to open and look out even when we feel boxed in. Our challenge is to become flexible enough and patient enough to let this happen.

Charles could have written those words, but he did more than that—he *lived* them! As we planned, I will stop by Thursday morning.

Dear Bev,

Since we spoke you have been in my meditations. The crushing pain of Jon's loss is now upon you. But death is not only about mourning; it is about truth.

When we have loved we always feel the grief of separation. But true understanding is the bridge between the experience of that suffering and the expression of our gratitude. You will only cease to weep when you cease looking for your beloved in the dark shadow of your own desires and begin to follow Jon by his own clear light.

Our suffering comes from the misconception that life begins with birth and ends with death. But there is only this moment, and in this moment there is neither beginning nor end. You told me that Jon died with a smile on his face. How lovely for him. The soul leaves the body in this way, with bliss and joy and light, only when its teachings on earth are complete for this lifetime.

In the midst of your anguish, try to keep in your heart that whatever has been given belongs to God. Remember that you were related to Jon through love, not through ownership. Everything is a "divine loan," while God still remains the owner of it. One is unburdened by allowing it all to be given back. Jon was with you as a reminder of God's blessings and teachings. When you remember Jon with love, you remember God.

With deepest respects,

Holland-born priest Henri J. M. Nouwen wrote a long letter of condolence to his father after the death of the priest's mother. It was later published in *A Letter of Consolation.* The following is an excerpt:

Dear Father,

Real grief is not healed by time. It is false to think that the passing of time will slowly make us forget her and take away our pain. I really want to console you in this letter, but not by suggesting that time will take away your pain, and that in one, two, three, or more years you will not miss her so much anymore.

I would not only be telling a lie, I would be diminishing the importance of mother's life, underestimating the depth of your grief, and mistakenly relativizing the power of the love that has bound mother and you together for forty-seven years. If time does anything, it deepens our grief. The longer we live, the more fully we become aware of who she was for us, and the more intimately we experience what her love meant for us. Real, deep love is, as you know, very unobtrusive, seemingly easy and obvious, and so present that we take it for granted. Therefore, it is often only in retrospect—or better, in memory—that we fully realize its power and depth. Yes, indeed, love often makes itself visible in pain. The pain we are now experiencing shows us how deep, full, intimate, and all-pervasive her love was.

Is this a consolation? Does this bring comfort? It appears that I am doing the opposite of bringing consolation. Maybe so. Maybe these words will only increase your tears and deepen your grief. But for me, your son, who grieves with you, there is no other way. I want to comfort and console you, but not in a way that covers up real pain and avoids all wounds. I am writing you this letter in the firm conviction that reality can be faced and entered with an open mind and an open heart, and in the sincere belief that consolation and comfort are to be found where our wounds hurt most.

'Abdu'l-Baha, son of the Prophet founder and head of the Baha'i faith from 1892 to 1921, wrote a letter to parents upon the death of their son. The following excerpt is taken from *Selections from the Writings of 'Abdu'l-Baha*, pages 199 to 200.

O ye two patient souls! Your letter was received. The death of that beloved youth and his separation from you have caused the utmost sorrow and grief; for he winged his flight in the flower of his age and the bloom of his youth to the heavenly nest. But he hath been freed from this sorrow-stricken shelter and hath turned his face toward the ever-lasting nest of the Kingdom, and, being delivered from a dark and narrow world, hath hastened to the sanctified realm of light; therein lieth the consolation of our hearts.

The inscrutable divine wisdom underlieth such heart-rending occurrences. It is as if a kind gardener transferreth a fresh and tender shrub from a confined place to a wide open area. This transfer is not the cause of the withering, the lessening or the destruction of that shrub; nay, on the contrary, it maketh it to grow and thrive, acquire freshness and delicacy, become green and bear fruit. This hidden secret is well known to the gardener, but those souls who are unaware of this bounty suppose that the gardener, in his anger and wrath, hath uprooted the shrub. Yet to those who are aware, this concealed fact is manifest, and this predestined decree is considered a bounty. Do not feel grieved or disconsolate, therefore, at the ascension of that bird of faithfulness.

More than a hundred years ago, a staret (spiritual director) of the Russian Orthodox Church, Ivanov Macarius, wrote this letter to a recently widowed woman:

> My Dearest Madame,
>
> I thank you for having unveiled to me the sadness of your grief-stricken heart; a great radiance comes over me when I share with others their sorrow. Complete, perfect, detailed compassion is the only answer I can give to your tender love of me that has led you, at such a time, to seek me out in my distant, silent, humble hermitage.
>
> . . . In the ground of the Christian's heart, sorrow for the dead soon melts, illuminated by the light of the true wisdom. Then, in the place of the vanished grief, there shoots up a new knowledge made of hope and faith. This knowledge does not only wash the soul of all sadness; it makes it glad.
>
> Fanaticism shackles the mind; faith gives it the wings of freedom. This freedom is apparent in a quiet firmness, unruffled by any circumstances, fortunate or unfortunate. The sword that cuts us free of shackles is the purified mind; the mind that has learnt to discern the true, the secret, the mysterious cause and purpose of every occurrence.

BUSINESS ORGANIZATIONS

In reviewing the available literature, we have been dismayed at the treatment of the issue of condolence in the workplace by some authorities. Among other things, these resources sometimes discourage interpersonal contact. For example, George Mazzei wrote the following in *The New Office Etiquette* (Poseidon, 1983):

> If a co-worker has a death in the family, it is an occasion for group condolences, and even a gift of flowers if the company pays for it. Verbal condolences among co-workers can be avoided if a note is sent. It is often awkward for a person to speak condolences to a grieving co-worker, and a card is the best way to handle it. (p. 93)

Upon the death of a co-worker, the shared grief of colleagues is often palpable and may impede the day-to-day workings of the business for some weeks. Along with assistance to the deceased's family, organizations sensitive to this situation may offer a memorial service in the workplace, time off for those who wish to attend the funeral, even referral to appropriate employee assistance programs for those who feel the need. On the positive side, this can be an opportunity for mutual support that will bring co-workers together and may enhance coping.

Employees will respond differently in their grief. For example, they may be irritable, distracted, or withdrawn or may overload themselves with work in an effort to block out painful feelings. A discussion of grief is found beginning on page 9.

Whether the situation involves the death of an employee or the death of an employee's loved one, the same principles discussed in Parts IV and V are equally applicable to condolence in the workplace. This chapter focuses on the special etiquette and issues involved in business letters of condolence. For management, a letter written to a bereaved employee or the loved ones of an employee who has died is an opportunity not only to express sincere sympathy but to communicate the concern of a sensitive, responsive, and caring firm.

A meaningful business letter of condolence has a distinct character and reflects the personality of the firm it represents. Unfortunately, a letter to the loved ones of a deceased employee or an employee in mourning is far too often a set piece, a boiler plate expression of cool sympathy. It should not be.

A thoughtful business letter of condolence, whether written from a sense of professional obligation or heartfelt sympathy, will be interpreted at three different levels. First, it carries a message of personal and group sympathy. Second, it is a permanent statement recognizing the value of the deceased or the bereaved to the firm and, in a larger sense, as a productive member of society. Third, unlike most personal sympathy letters, a letter that comes from an employer may be shown to many. As such, it serves as a vital public relations statement with the potential to spread goodwill and cast the image of the firm in a positive light.

1. *Because it represents the firm, this letter must be in impeccable business form, carefully proofread and balanced aesthetically on the page.* This is an exception to the strong suggestion that letters of condolence should be handwritten.

2. *It is important to remember that a letter of condolence from anyone in a firm, other than a close personal friend, represents the entire company.* The writer's official position in the company's hierarchy also communicates a secondary message to the bereaved. Consider that it is the president of the United States who signs each letter of condolence upon the death of a member of the military.

3. *The letter should be given careful attention to assure that it is not stilted, rigid, or unnecessarily formal but well-crafted and personal.* While it should be complimentary, it must not fall into the trap of overstatement in an attempt to compensate for what may be a lack of positive recognition in the past. This is an opportunity to let the bereaved know how appreciated their loved one was in the workplace.

4. *Use the letter to highlight aspects of the employee's character, personality, or skills and to document the deceased's contributions to the business.* Anecdotes are particularly apt; they create a beau-

tiful visual memory of the employee at work for the bereaved to cherish.

5. *If appropriate, the business may take this opportunity to offer its assistance in very specific ways* (e.g., sorting out personal effects; reviewing pension, insurance, and other work-related legal documents; financial assistance; help with correspondence or establishing credit). Many business letters of condolence include the name and phone number of a contact person at the firm designated to coordinate help. This can be very reassuring to the bereaved.

6. *When it is not the employee but the loved one of an employee who has died, the thoughtful company will always respond with a letter.* Here, the opportunity is to take an extra step by expressing support and understanding for the bereaved employee.

LETTERS OF CONDOLENCE FROM BUSINESSES AND ORGANIZATIONS

Dear Dr. Robinson,

We at the Army Corps of Engineers were shocked and deeply saddened by the news of Gregory's passing. Gregory had worked with us for many years and he contributed significantly to our nationwide program for the Corps of Engineers. He made many major contributions to the Corps' project studies and training program and he was an outstanding credit to the engineering profession. Your husband was a uniquely wonderful person to work with, always full of energy and enthusiasm. His wit and vitality provided our meetings, project briefings, and training courses with a special spark that ignited imaginations and opened our minds to good clear communication.

We will miss Gregory's engineering excellence throughout the Corps of Engineers, but more significantly, we will miss Gregory's energy, his cheerful spirit, his "can-do" attitude toward work and challenges, his willingness to contribute, advise, and assist, and most of all, his wonderful friendship.

We at the Army Corps of Engineers wanted you and your family to know that Gregory meant a great deal to a lot of people in this country. We will all miss him terribly. If you ever need help in any way, please call on us. Jim McCullough of our staff has volunteered to be our contact person. Please call us any time at (813) 786-9831.

We are all very sorry.

Dear Mr. and Mrs. Patton,

It is with a heavy heart that I write to express deep sympathy to you and your family upon the death of your son. All of us here at Newland and Goldstein share your loss, for Matthew Patton was long a well-loved and highly respected member of our firm. He will be greatly missed.

In his seven years with our organization, I considered Matthew to be one of the best advertising writers I have ever known. He was original and imaginative, full of ideas, incisive, and forward-thinking.

Perhaps the one quality to commend him most was his unfailing enthusiasm for the job at hand—an enthusiasm that naturally transmitted itself to those who worked with him.

I know that words can do little to ease your burden of sorrow, but perhaps the affection and cherished memories of Matt's many friends and associates here may give you some small measure of comfort. That is what we are all hoping.

Andrew Schneider, our vice-president, will be calling in a few days to explain the life insurance and profit-sharing benefits that Matt had designated for you. If there is any other way that we can be of service at this difficult time, please let Mr. Schneider know.

Cordially,

Dear Mrs. Hartford,

The Board of Directors has requested that I express to you their profound sympathy upon the death of your husband, Jack.

All of us at Sloane and Associates valued Jack's insights, his determination, his creativity, and we were inspired by his enthusiasm for life. Most important, he will be remembered by all of us for his genuine concern for others.

We grieve with you at his passing, and feel grateful for having known him.

With deepest sympathy,

The following is a letter to an employee on the death of his wife.

Dear Ted,

The entire department was shocked and saddened to hear about the accident and Marilyn's death. I have such a fond memory of meeting her first at the organizational dinner two years back. She struck me as warm, vivacious, and intelligent and we talked of your plans to move into the position you now hold. Watching the two of you and recalling some of the things you've said about her, I know she must have provided inspiration, meaning, and emotional support in so many of your career accomplishments.

Bill Satterfield has asked if he might speak with you later this week to sort out what needs to be done during your absence to keep things running smoothly for you at work. He'll give you a call before coming by.

Those of us here at the office want to express our sympathy by making a contribution in Marilyn's name to the American Heart Association.

We hope that time will bring cherished memories to take the place of your present sorrow.

Sincerely,

Chapter 10

Upon the Death of a Pet

> LOS ANGELES (AP)—Perhaps all dogs go to heaven, but few make the trip in a silk-lined casket like Skippy, the house pet killed by a gun-toting mailman.
>
> Funeral arrangements for the two-year-old German shepherd include the plush casket, large floral displays, a graveside ceremony and a headstone to mark his resting place at a pet cemetery, officials said Thursday.

Society is beginning to accept the loss of a dog, cat, or other loved and cherished pet as a grief-filled experience. The increasing popularity of pet cemeteries attests to this fact. The arrangements may be new, but the sentiments are not. Long before the prevalence of today's pet cemeteries, Queen Victoria of Great Britain dedicated a special resting place for the pets of military men serving at Edinburgh Castle. President Franklin Delano Roosevelt chose to be buried next to his beloved dog Fala at their home in Hyde Park, New York.

Bereavement following the loss of a pet may seem inappropriate to some, but it is no light matter to thousands of animal lovers. Animals are protectors and fast friends to the young, valued family members and cheering companions to the elderly. They are confidants to singles, they soothe prison inmates, and they gladden the lives of many who are institutionalized.

Great sadness, pain, and grief often follow the death of an animal. Since deep attachments are frequently established with pets, strong emotional responses to their deaths are neither abnormal nor inappropriate. Those who experience the death of a pet may grieve as much as they would for the loss of a family member or close friend. But since society generally agrees that a human bond is more meaningful than that with an animal, many bereaved pet owners experience bewilderment, embarrassment, and guilt over the depth of their grief experience.

On the other hand, the death of a pet offers a beautiful opportunity to educate children in the naturalness of death and the healing grief process. For children, the death of a pet is often their first encounter with loss through death, and many children exhibit the emotions that we expect following human loss. In moving through shock, denial, anger, guilt, loneliness, and other emotions, the child has a direct experience of bereavement. This encounter can actually aid growth and begins to provide a healthy foundation for coping with loss later in life.

Many children conduct secret burials for their pets. If discovered, it is important that parents don't diminish the importance of the event to the child. If the family chooses to hold a funeral, the ceremony may provide both children and adults with an opportunity to ask questions and express painful and sensitive emotions. A pet's funeral can include eulogizing, singing, and prayer. Through this ritual, children come face to face with the beauty of caring, the pain of letting go, and the finality of death.

The elderly are another group for whom the death of a much loved animal presents a unique situation. Seniors frequently form close bonds with their pets, some of whom have been with their owners for many years. These relationships often ease loneliness at a time when human relationships have fallen away. Animal companions serve as facilitators for social interactions, trained helpers, and protectors. Most importantly, the unconditional love of animals can be a loving support and enhancer of self-esteem. So deep may be their grief that sometimes, after the death of a pet, the elderly who are alone express suicidal feelings or wishes for death:

> When my wife died nearly ten years ago it was terrible. I had friends and the kids, of course, but it was Rusty who stayed by me night and day. He seemed to know just what had happened and I felt like we both missed her.
>
> This year, Rusty had to be put to sleep and I know people would think I'm crazy, but sometimes I just wish they'd do the same for me. It's so lonely out here and I just can't seem to get over it.

A warm-hearted visit or a letter of condolence will not only be a much appreciated and welcome surprise but will help the bereaved recognize that their grieving is understood and is natural.

1. *Grief that follows the death of a pet is often suppressed by bereaved who feel that others will think they are foolish.* This may prompt avoidance of those who the bereaved feel will be insensitive to their loss.

2. *The death of a pet frequently triggers aftershocks of grief from previous losses.* It may rekindle and be complicated by expressions of unresolved grief, confusing both the mourner and friends who wish to help.

3. *Euthanasia is often a consideration facing the owner of an elderly or ailing pet.* This difficult decision, no matter how clear-cut the situation may appear to others, is usually fraught with painful ambivalence and guilt. Sensitivity is the key here. Whatever your personal opinion about pet euthanasia, try to respect that others may see the world differently. If the pet owner makes a choice to proceed with euthanasia and you support it, you can bring great comfort by acknowledging the difficulty of the decision and the rightness of giving merciful release from a body that no longer functions.

4. *As with other losses, following the death of a loved pet avoid insensitive comments.* Examples include, "It was just a cat. Why don't you get another one?" or "It's foolish to cry."

5. *Children who have been their pet's primary caretakers may experience guilt over the death of the animal.* Inconsistency in pet

care is a typical pattern for youngsters. Children need reassurance that their real or imagined irresponsibilities have not led to a pet's death.

LETTERS OF CONDOLENCE UPON THE DEATH OF A PET

Dear Kelly,

I want to tell you how sorry I was to hear of the death of your wonderful companion, Chipper. He was a great friend and you were some pair of playmates for each other. But more than that, Chipper had a beautiful soul, a warm heart, and a caring quality that made him a very special dog.

It's a hard blow for you and at this sad time I want you to know that you have my sincere sympathy.

Love,
Joanie

Dear Snowdens,

We want to express our sympathy upon the death of your sweet cat today. After speaking with Mark it was apparent that the decision to ease her final days wasn't easy.

Jane and I know that your family pet was deeply loved for many years. Cats are such independent creatures; we never quite know if they are going to let us into their world. But when they do, they allow us to love them unconditionally, and the loss of a loved one is always painful. Of course, not everyone, especially those who have never shared their home with a pet, will understand your sadness, but the sadness is there nonetheless.

We hope you will give yourselves permission to feel the grief. Thinking of you.

Sincerely,
Larry and Janet

The following is from *The Letters of Edith Wharton,* edited by R.W.B. Lewis and Nancy Lewis (Scribner's, 1989).

Small dogs, a long succession of them, were the joy and solace of Edith Wharton's life. Their loss afflicted her hardly less than that of much loved humans, and she was sure that other dog lovers felt the same. Here she condoles with Charles Eliot Norton . . . the death of his dog Taffy.

June 30 [1908]

Dear Mr. Norton,

When Teddy & I heard yesterday from Lily (Norton's daughter Elizabeth) of Taffy's sad taking-off we both really felt a personal regret in addition to our profound sympathy for his master.

His artless but engaging ways, his candid enjoyment of his dinner, his judicious habit of exercising by means of those daily rushes up and down the road, had for so many years interested and attracted us that he occupies a very special place in our crowded dog-memories.

As for your feelings, I can picture them with intensity, since to do so I have only to relive my poor Jules' last hours and farewell looks, about a year ago!

Somebody says "L'espoir est le plus fidele des amants" ("Hope is the most faithful of lovers")—but I really think it should be put in the plural and applied to dogs. Staunch and faithful little lovers that they are, they give back a hundred fold every sign of love one ever gives them—and it mitigates the pang of losing them to know how very happy a little affection has made them.

While representing the Colonies in England, Benjamin Franklin came to know the family of Jonathan Shipley, a member of the House of Lords. He befriended the young Miss Georgiana Shipley, and later he and his wife sent her a gift from America, Mungo, a pet squirrel. This letter was written upon Franklin's learning of Mungo's death when Georgiana was sixteen. It is particularly interesting not only for the touchingly playful tone but historically for the closing verse of the epitaph; the American Revolution was still several years in the future.

London, September 26, 1772

Dear Miss,

I lament with you most sincerely the unfortunate end of poor *Mungo.* Few squirrels were better accomplished; for he had had a good education, had traveled far, and seen much of the world. As he had the honour of being, for his virtues, your favourite, he should not go, like common skuggs, without an elegy or an epitaph. Let us give him one in the monumental style and measure, which, being neither prose nor verse, is perhaps the properest for grief; since to use common language would look as if we were not affected, and to make rhymes would seem trifling in sorrow.

Epitaph

Alas! poor Mungo!
Happy wert thou, hadst thou known
Thy own felicity.
Remote from the fierce bald eagle,
Tyrant of thy native woods,
Thou hadst nought to fear from his piercing talons,
Nor from the murdering gun
Of the thoughtless sportsman.
Safe in thy wired castle,
Grimalkin never could annoy thee.
Daily wert thou fed with the choicest viands.
By the fair hand of an indulgent mistress;
But, discontented,
Thou wouldst have more freedom.
Too soon, alas! didst thou obtain it;
And wandering,
Thou art fallen by the fangs of wanton, cruel Ranger!
Learn hence,
Ye who blindly seek more liberty,
Whether subjects, sons, squirrels or daughters,
That apparent restraint may be real protection;

Yielding peace and plenty
With security.

You see, my dear Miss, how much more decent and proper this broken style is, than if we were to say, by way of epitaph,

Here Skugg
Lies snug,
As a bug
In a rug.

And yet, perhaps, there are people in the world of so little feeling as to think that this would be a good-enough epitaph for poor Mungo.

If you wish it, I shall procure another to succeed him; but perhaps you will now choose some other amusement.

Remember me affectionately to all the good family, and believe me ever,

Your affectionate friend,
B. Franklin

Part IV

What Can I Say?

Give sorrow words; the grief that
does not speak
Whispers the o'er-fraught heart
and bids it break.

—MACBETH, Act IV, sc. 3

Chapter 11

Allowing What Is

We hear it time and again. The most common concern and frequently the most common roadblock for those who wish to condole are the five simple words, "I never know what to say."

We feel so inept. No matter how erudite we typically consider ourselves, no matter how much we love words, the limitations of our spoken language become glaring in the face of grief. Frustration often follows. Our hearts are so full, yet words seem so small.

Why is it that our deepest emotions are the most difficult to express in words? Think about it. Young lovers, swept away in the blush of first love, stare into one another's eyes and say nothing. Anger deafens a room without speaking a word. Loneliness often retreats into a mournful, gray silence. An ancient saying suggests that "Truth cannot be said in words." It seems that when our feelings are most powerful and most true, words—at least for a time—fall short.

How awkward the silences feel. Our first tendency is often to fill them with small talk, more out of our own discomfort than for the benefit of the mourner. But the sensitive consoler soon learns that "what to say" begins in the language of silence—in just being there. This chapter sets the scene for healing conversation. The chapter that follows deals with suggestions to assist you in beginning a dialogue with the bereaved. But before you can really speak from the heart, you need to bring your full awareness to the moment.

BEING THERE

To be there, to listen, to accept, these are the first gifts we can offer each other in times of loss. In an article on grief by Jo Coudert in *Woman's Day* magazine (May 10, 1988) the author perceptively observes, "You can't talk people out of despair, but you can be there with them and for them."

We asked a good friend what it was that helped most during his bereavement. His answer came without hesitation:

> It was simply knowing that good friends were available if I needed them. Even when I was nearly paralyzed with emotional pain, I knew that there were a few people who I could count on to be there. No judgments, maybe even no words, just being there in a way that reminded me that I was alive and that life would go on. Their presence was a lifeline.

There are resources available throughout our lives that we rarely use. Some of these are material; others come in the form of friends, relations, and business professionals. Our own vast inner resources often go untapped until we are faced with either a personal crisis or one that touches the life of a friend. As condolers we reach deeply and sometimes, to our surprise, find strength and courage and compassion.

Now "being there" does not necessarily mean being continually physically present. Rather, it means communicating an attitude of availability that is authentic. Keep in mind that this availability becomes more, not less, important over time. Especially in the first days of grief, your presence and gracious offers to help are often seen only through a cloud of numbness and pain. In subsequent days and weeks, when many who sent their initial sympathies have returned to their everyday lives, mourners are often left to their own devices by these "condolence dropouts." How do you make known your availability? Simple. You offer periodic reminders in the form of notes, phone calls, or visits.

After the death of his father, a divorced forty-one-year-old school counselor explained his loneliness in the weeks following the funeral:

> I'd returned to work and the days were all right, I guess. I had other people's problems to think about. But my evenings and weekends were another matter. I suppose my friends didn't realize how desperately I needed to hear from them, and I was too uncomfortable to let them know. They probably felt they were doing the right thing, not wanting to impose at a private time. But I'll tell you, it would have been anything but an imposition. In my grief, I interpreted their good intentions as a lack of concern; I guess I'm still not sure.

Rabbi Pesach Krauss and Morrie Goldfischer, in their sensitive book, *Why Me?*, put it this way:

> A mourner feels his greatest despair after sympathetic visitors disperse. His house is empty and his evenings frequently dreary and unbearable. That's when the steadfast friend who is there for the long haul fulfills the greatest need. His contribution goes far beyond his presence, important as it is. By being there, he encourages his friend to express his anger, guilt, and depression, and to openly shed his tears. (p. 133)

Once again, being there doesn't mean that you are obligated to stay with a grieving friend for endless hours or respond to every request that might be made of you. Bereavement is a very difficult life transition. Those in grief may seem detached and unappreciative or demanding and insensitive to your own time commitments. You can be sympathetic, supportive, and available, but you can't take away someone else's pain or become their personal savior.

ACCEPTANCE AND REASSURANCE

Being there is one thing. Being there in total acceptance is another. Acceptance of life *as it is* has always been one of the hallmarks of spirituality. It is an expression of trust in the "rightness" of existence. Acceptance is one of the most important gifts you can give to someone in grief. This means a full, complete, and nonjudgmental allowing of the person's feelings, thoughts, attitudes, and behaviors.

Those in grief struggle moment by moment with discomfort and anxiety as they experience the many intense manifestations of mourning. Tears, rage, protest, memory lapses, and an inability to complete the simplest tasks often provoke embarrassment. However their inner pain is communicated—explosive outbursts, silence, or pleading with God—it is helpful if you can allow their expression of anguish in these pivotal moments of their life.

Doug Manning, a minister and an authority on bereavement, tells the story of a young mother in acute grief. Those around her, witnessing her outpouring of tears, suggested that she "get a hold" of herself. In her response, the disconsolate woman uttered the words that gave Manning the title for his book, *Don't Take My Grief Away.* Deeply moved by her spontaneous plea, Manning wrote:

> Her words have [also] done more to change my concept of grief and recovery than any words I have ever heard. I wondered how many times I had tried to take grief away from folks. How many times I had denied them the right to grieve in my presence because I made it quite clear I would not accept such activity. (p. 62)

If those in grief are going to open to their hearts, if they are going to be successful in releasing their pain, if they are going to accept the risk of voicing irrational thoughts, they need your full acceptance. Avoid statements such as "Get a grip on yourself," "It's not the time for you to fall apart," or "Be strong for the children." At an airport we couldn't help but overhear the conversation of a couple waiting on line just in front of us. The woman softly suggested to her husband, "Just calm down; it'll be all right," to which he snapped in response, "It's *my* father who's dead and it isn't all right."

Your acceptance is of service in two crucial ways. First, it allows the expression of the experience of grief. This is vital to the healing process (see Chapter 2, The Phases of Grief). Second, it validates the naturalness of the bereaved's response. Mourners often feel themselves going "over the edge." The intensity of their emotions frequently causes them to question their normalcy. A few words may go a long way toward reassuring the bereaved that their feelings, no matter how strange they seem, are natural. Verbal reassurances include statements such as "I can only imagine how much pain you must be feeling," or "It seems so natural to cry at a time like this." You may also want to assure the bereaved of your continuing presence, making clear that, while you wish to stay, you will leave without feeling insulted if they so desire.

Whatever length of time you are present, a quality of patience is golden. It means not being in a hurry, not being annoyed, not being demanding, and most importantly, not forcing things. Healing cannot be forced and you serve best when you are a witness to healing, perhaps a catalyst, but not a prodder.

THE POWER OF TOUCH

When words fail or when silence speaks more eloquently, simply consider taking your friend gently by the hand, touching his shoulder or embracing him. Let this gesture speak for you; your friend or loved one will most probably understand well your message of caring. Be sensitive, however, and if the bereaved seems to be uncomfortable with your physical gesture, respect this communication, be it verbal or nonverbal. Try not to take any irritability, anger, or rejection personally. These responses are common in bereavement.

Metaphors employing touch are a regular part of our vocabulary. We say we are "touched" when strong and tender feelings are experienced. Of an unpredictable and changing situation we say "it was touch and go." The lowest caste in

India's socioreligious structure is called the "untouchables." When a loved one goes out of our life, we "lose touch." This symbolic expression reflects the harsh reality of a departure at a physical level.

Many bereaved individuals relate that they have received comfort in the loving touches and hugs of relatives and friends. It's as if such actions are a tangible source of strength and reassurance. These observations even come from people who are not ordinarily "touchers." Consider the power of touch as expressed in these examples:

> After the first flurry of activity diminished, I still welcomed a firm hand clasp or a hug. I couldn't say that to anyone; it would be too embarrassing. Somehow, I never wanted to appear needy in any way. But a genuine touch from a friend was often a reminder that, yes, there truly were others out there who cared. I needed that reminder for a long time.

> For several weeks after the funeral I don't recall anyone touching me except tentatively, so tentatively it made me uncomfortable. Then one afternoon several friends from Bob's office came over after work. His boss, who, I had heard, had been visibly shaken following the accident, took my hand for a moment. I will never forget that moment. I felt his pain, his compassion, and his sorrow. A moment before I was not aware of my hand and now a thousand words were spoken through touch. It was a first step out of my shell. The dark cloud of grief opened for a moment and, for the first time, I knew other moments would follow.

What is it about touch during grief that is so healing? First, touch helps the bereaved remember that they exist by breaking through the cocoon of numbness that so often accompanies the first stages of grief. Second, the sensitive physical touch of a friend reminds the bereaved that others will want to touch them again, that they are not cut off from humanity. Those in acute grief often feel undesirable and untouchable. Sometimes, by just receiving a caring touch, something relaxes in the body.

Finally, the touch of someone with an open heart has an intangible healing quality all its own. The benefit of a "laying on of hands" has been recognized since ancient times as having transformative healing power. Touch is truly a forgotten language, and in the silences that so frequently accompany grief, it can be the single most powerful means of communication.

Chapter 12

Conversational Hints

SWIFT TO HEAR, SLOW TO SPEAK

> Therefore, my beloved brethren, let every man be swift to hear, slow to speak.
>
> —JAMES 1:19

It may seem odd or at least curious that a discussion of conversational hints should begin with the theme of listening, not speaking. Yet, the notion that condolence means only speaking meaningfully to the bereaved is misguided. In the previous chapter we focused on the significance of "being there" to console a friend. Having said that, and if we truly wish to respond to the needs of those in grief, our condoling actions will typically begin with a distinct emphasis on listening, not talking.

There is a power and a beauty in the silence of listening. There's also a clear message, "I'm right here. I care and I'm with you. I'm not sure what to say, but I'm ready to listen." A very delicate alertness is needed for authentic listening. The art requires ears, of course, but the real listening comes from the heart because that is where sympathy and healing begin. It is a silent way of sharing in the mourning, but it is also a way of helping the bereaved to find their own solutions. A retired cardiovascular surgeon, W. Sterling Edwards, M.D., in an article for the *American Medical News,* noted after beginning to study the art of listening:

> To listen deeply for the expressor's feelings takes energy, but the effect is often amazing. When someone realizes that

> another individual is truly listening empathically, the emotional flood gates may open with the release of pent-up feelings. And, if this deep listening continues, the speaker often comes up with his or her own solutions to problems, which are so much better than solutions advised by others. (October 20, 1989, p. 43)

Most people in grief have a desire that sometimes approaches a compulsion to talk about what has happened to them. While some bereaved may withdraw from verbal contact altogether, and others experience this inner urge to talk almost continuously, for most, the nearly desperate need to communicate verbally ebbs and flows for weeks or months. As these mourners experience powerful emotions and uncommon sensations, they often feel that they're going to "lose control," "fall apart," or "go crazy" if they can't tell someone what they're going through. They need to talk and, at times, they vitally need someone to listen and then to reassure them of the normalcy of their thoughts. Often, the story of their loss and memories surrounding it are repeated over and over as part of the healing process. This may surprise, annoy, and tire friends while frightening the bereaved. But such repetitive talking accomplishes two psychological tasks: It helps the bereaved confront the reality of the loss in deeper and deeper ways, and it is one important natural process by which the bereaved continue to hold on to their loved one.

The bereaved need to be listened to, not supplied with answers. They know deep down that there are no explanations to the most important questions they are asking themselves, and they aren't really expecting answers from those who console them. Mourning has to be lived through; it cannot be resolved with intellectual responses. Being an accepting and caring presence and a good listener is one of the greatest gifts one person can give to another in grief.

Despite understanding that listening performs a vital function in condolence, few people can listen to another's sorrow without sometimes feeling anxiety or discomfort. Why is this so? First, while the bereaved's loss has the power to enlighten our ability as consolers, it may also put us in touch with our own unresolved feelings of grief and sadness. The key word is *unresolved,* because if we have worked through our own losses this is not likely to occur. Second, listeners often experience feelings of inadequacy that arise out of their not knowing how to respond. They fear that if they have no answers or words of wisdom, they will be of no help at all. Third, many feel an uncomfortable and unwarranted sense of obligation to share their own intimate experiences of loss. Such disclosure, they assume, may create more familiarity than is desired.

Some condolers resolve their discomfort by simply removing themselves physically from the presence of the bereaved. An embarrassed but honest woman recounted how once, upon leaving for a condolence visit, she'd arranged to receive a telephone call ten minutes after her arrival. When the call came, she informed the bereaved that her presence was urgently required elsewhere and swiftly made her exit. After some discussion, the same woman went on to explain that her parents had died in a fire several years before and she had never allowed herself to grieve for them. Since that time, she'd found that listening to the grief of others caused her extreme tension.

Of course one needn't leave the room to avoid authentic listening. Some condolers remain with the bereaved, but avoid having to listen in other ways. When confronted by an intimate sharing on the part of the mourner, "avoidant" condolers may change the subject ("Let me get you a cool drink"), participate in or encourage participation in distracting activities ("I'll clean up the kitchen; you just go on and keep talking"), or make patronizing remarks that stifle the bereaved's grief ("Why are you torturing yourself by going over and over it?"; "It's time to stop crying"; "I never thought I'd see you like this").

If these scenarios seem familiar to you, don't be disheartened. Listening is an art and a skill and learning a few approaches can enhance one's way of relating to others, whether condoling or in general conversation.

SUGGESTIONS FOR POSITIVE AND HEALING COMMUNICATION

It's not uncommon to be fearful of saying the wrong thing to a friend in grief. As a result, many would-be condolers withdraw or hold back rather than reach out. They tell themselves they're doing this to respect the bereaved's privacy, but it is rarely the truth. Usually, they are just taking the easy way out.

As you approach and begin to converse with the bereaved, certainly there is a risk, but as Dr. Zunin points out in his book *Contact: The First Four Minutes,* "Human contact is always a challenge . . . which means a certain amount of risk-taking . . . an investment that earns interest in love, friendship, growth and a more positive self-image," both for the condoler and the bereaved. People in crisis often need others around them, but it may not always be evident to them or to those who care for them. With care and sensitivity your presence can be a gift, not a burden.

Once you have taken the time to listen, healing conversation can begin. Here are a few remarks you may find helpful in getting started:

I'm so sorry. Was your father ill for a long time?

I am at a loss to know what to say, but I sense how very difficult this must be for you.

I've been thinking about you and wanted to know how (what) you've been doing.

This must be a bewildering and incredibly complicated time. It must be very hard for you (and your family).

What's it like for you these days? How are you coping?

Do you feel like talking for a while?

The following are suggestions for continued positive communication with those in grief. They may not only help you to avoid pitfalls, but they may help you to overcome some realistic concerns.

1. *Perhaps another time.* Even though you may be totally prepared to listen, the time may not be right. Don't burden the bereaved because you have decided you are ready and willing to listen. If you are caring, receptive, and patient the time will eventually present itself.

2. *Listen without judgment.* Don't prejudge; don't moralize; don't condemn. Though there will be times when what the person is feeling seems to you to be inaccurate or inappropriate, don't tell the bereaved how or what they should be feeling. The really attentive listener remains alert, present, receptive, and avoids drawing conclusions.

3. *Focus your attention.* Concentrate on the person and what is being said by giving your undivided attention. This does not mean being silently impatient or apathetically quiet. And try not to think about what you're going to say as soon as the other person stops talking. Such nonverbal cues as maintaining good eye contact, leaning forward, nodding your head affirmatively, and using facial expressions indicate encouragement and confirm your attentiveness.

4. *Avoid interrupting.* Allow the bereaved to complete their sentences and their thoughts even though the words may seem confused or fragmented. Try not to jump in at any opening, finish a statement, or hurry the bereaved along. In addition, when we suggest that you avoid interrupting, we mean not only the bereaved's words but their silences as well. The silence of grief can be remarkably eloquent.

5. *Maintain a positive outlook on life.* Conversing with the bereaved doesn't always mean discussing pain and sorrow. Be attuned to what they want to talk about. There will be times when the bereaved want to discuss ordinary things and other times when they wish to share some of their anguish. It is immensely helpful if you can maintain a positive outlook on life and a quality of affirmation. Your attitude will be con-

veyed in many subtle ways, especially by supporting the bereaved in whatever they are feeling. You might also talk about how either the bereaved or the deceased has touched, enriched, or even inspired your life. Mention the positive qualities and strengths you and others have noticed about them or relate memories that you cherish.

6. *Rational answers are irrational.* The death of a loved one can never be explained away with logic. Don't try. It rarely helps to offer "rational" explanations about death to someone in grief.

7. *Suggestions are better than advice.* Grief is an intensely personal experience. The true friend is one who does not advise but helps the other to become more alert, more aware, and more conscious of life's choices. You may offer some gentle suggestions, but do so without the mantle of authority or demand. Instead, help the bereaved to find their own way with courage and authenticity.

8. *Share, don't compare, experiences.* Those in the early stages of grief often feel their situation is so unique that no one can understand. They will be put off and shut off by any suggestion that your experience—or the experience of others you know—has been more intense or more profound. If you choose to discuss your own experiences with grief, share without comparing or professing complete understanding. The bereaved may find comfort, understanding, or ways of coping when you share your own experiences in this manner.

Another area in which one-upmanship may cause problems occurs when the condoler suggests that his or her love for the deceased was as great, if not greater, than that of the bereaved. Use judgment in sharing such feelings; the newly bereaved are highly vulnerable.

9. *Give occasional responses while listening.* There are many ways of conveying that you are engaged, that you understand, or that you want to know more:

- Soft, affirming conversational sounds that we all use without thinking (hmmm, uh huh) denote interest, agreement, and concern.
- Asking for clarification, whether in the form of questioning, repeating, or paraphrasing, checks to see that you've understood what the bereaved has said (e.g., if the bereaved mentions that she doesn't know how she's going to get to her doctor's appointment, the condoler might respond by asking, "Would you like me to give you a lift?").
- Simple requests for more information are helpful. While it's possible to ask for too much disclosure, most condolers err on the side of asking too little. Typically, the bereaved have a compelling need to talk about the who, what, when, and why of their loss. Inquiries may be general ("Tell me more about it") or specific ("How did you find out?").
- Reflective questioning is another way of encouraging the bereaved to talk. By occasionally repeating key words or phrases just spoken by the bereaved, you validate their remarks, demonstrate your attentiveness, and confirm your interest. (Bereaved: "I feel that I'm behaving like an angry ten-year-old kid." Condoler: "An angry ten-year-old?")

10. *Consider before using these remarks.* Many of the following reflect more about the condoler's own difficulty in coping with loss than about their sympathy for the bereaved:

Be thankful you have another child.

You must get on with your life.

You're not the first person this has happened to.

Don't cry; try to keep control of yourself.

You're young; there's plenty of time to have children.

I know exactly what you are going through.

It was really a blessing; you must be relieved.

You are lucky to have had him for so long.

Don't worry. It's probably for the best.

It's better this way.

It's a blessing in disguise.

He's better off this way; if he'd lived it would have been more painful for him.

Don't take it so hard.

Try to keep yourself together.

We have no right to question God's will.

Why didn't you call me?

I heard you're not taking it well.

It's just as well that you never got to know the baby.

Sensitivity is so important. When people share their suffering, they often feel vulnerable, foolish, and fearful that their self-disclosure will negatively impact your relationship with them. Often in grief there is a temporary impairment of self-esteem along with feelings of insecurity. The bereaved needs to know that no matter what is said, your friendship will remain intact. You will communicate simple acceptance and genuine caring with statements such as "I now more fully understand much of what you've been experiencing and I admire your courage and the difficult decisions you've made." Let the bereaved know you're really trying to understand what they are going through and that you respect how they are coping.

What follows is a specific format you may wish to consider in conversing with someone in grief. Its clear and simple structure has made it invaluable to many who never thought they would be truly comfortable talking with bereaved friends and loved ones.

A FOUR-STEP GUIDE: DEBRIEFING

Week after week the six o'clock news brings the reports into our homes. Along with weather and sports are frequent images of destruction on a scale almost too vast to take in. Whole villages disappear in Afghanistan. Freeways collapse in San Francisco. The Eastern seaboard is ripped apart by hurricanes and in California fires engulf hundreds of canyon homes. An airliner explodes and the world mourns. Night after night and with our morning coffee we are confronted by the devastation of property and the desperation of people faced with overwhelming loss.

In recent years, mental health professionals have become increasingly aware of the potentially devastating psychological effects that these disasters frequently have not only on survivors but on those who have been involved in emergency services during the crises. In the book *Disaster Work and Mental Health: Prevention and Control of Stress Among Workers* (National Institute of Mental Health) Diane Myers, R.N., M.S.N., addresses the far-reaching impact of this kind of personal and community upheaval:

> A disaster is an awesome event. Simply seeing massive destruction and terrible sights evokes deep feelings. Often, residents of disaster-stricken communities report disturbing feelings of grief, sadness, anxiety, and anger, even when they are not themselves victims of the disaster. . . . This is true for workers as well as community residents. (p. 72)

An increased awareness of this issue has led to the development of a new approach to help both survivors and those who help them to cope more effectively with the emotional turmoil that sometimes surfaces following such experiences. *Critical incident stress debriefing* (usually referred to as "debriefing") is the professional term for this new form of crisis intervention. The goal of this organized conversational approach is to eliminate, or at least minimize, delayed stress reactions and their physical and psychological toll.

Later in this section we outline our adaptation of this process, an approach to healing conversation we now call "A Four-Step Guide: Debriefing." Those who have used this framework tell us that it gives them the confidence to talk comfortably with those in grief. This has been the case with both the general public and professionals. In a workshop on loss given by Hilary Zunin, one teacher noted:

> I've always been afraid that I'd put my foot in my mouth if I reached out to someone in grief. But this four-step guide made sense from the start. I've begun responding with much more self-confidence and have been able to be there with my heart instead of listening to my mind busily wondering what to say next.

Following the San Francisco earthquake of October 17, 1989, Dr. Zunin was involved in debriefing those emotionally impacted by the event. These people did not lose loved ones, but nonetheless they were experiencing emotional aftershocks with which they couldn't cope. Some had experienced the loss of their homes and all their possessions; others were materially intact but for a variety of reasons found themselves deeply affected by the disaster.

Later, Dr. Zunin worked with other groups of "victims." He led debriefing groups for mental health volunteers who had helped survivors following the quake. In the course of this work, it became apparent that a number of the reactions of both actual earthquake survivors and those who had reached out to help them were understandably very similar to patterns of normal grief response.

A young physical therapist came to the mental health crisis center about three weeks after the quake. Although she hadn't been physically hurt, and she didn't know anyone who had been seriously injured, her home had sustained major damage. She'd lost several pounds in the time since the quake, but hadn't been too concerned about it. About a week after the event she'd gone back to work and was living at a friend's house. Things seemed to be going all right, yet soon after, recurrent nightmares had begun:

> It's always the same. I'm buried in rubble and can hardly breathe. I yell, but no one hears. I'm not exactly sure why

> I'm here, but I'm kind of losing it at work. I drift off for a while and then snap at people for no reason or burst into tears. And I shouldn't, you know; they've all been really great, supportive and right there for me. I feel like a fool.

This physical therapist and thousands like her who had their lives violently disrupted by the earthquake were experiencing features akin to normal grief. Working with debriefing made it clear to Dr. Zunin that the simple steps of this extremely effective approach could be used by anyone whose goal was to comfort in a time of loss.

In his article, "When Disaster Strikes" (*Journal of Emergency Medical Services,* January 1983, p. 33), Jeffrey T. Mitchell, originator of the term and the process, clarifies debriefing's central theme:

> The tone must be positive, supportive, and understanding. Everyone has feelings which need to be shared and accepted. The main rule is—no one criticizes another; all listen to what was, or is, going on inside each other.

Although Mitchell was referring to debriefing in groups, the principle applies equally to one-on-one interactions. When might you try this approach? It's usually not applicable in the hours immediately following notification of the death of a loved one. At that time, shock, disbelief, and an emotional outpouring typically preclude this kind of extended conversation. But from a couple of days to a couple of months, our adaptation of this process may be used either in the course of a single visit or during a series of conversations. One of the most positive aspects of the debriefing process is that it follows the natural evolution of a caring interaction about loss.

The simplicity of these four practical steps may be deceiving. First, you need to be prepared to listen authentically. Then, once your ears and heart are open, the practice of this process can have enormous value in providing comfort and support in the face of loss.

1. *Ask about the facts.* Especially in the early stages of grief it is easier for most bereaved to talk about facts rather than feelings. Those in grief are likely to be preoccupied; they are disconnected from their feelings and may be irritated, confused, and uncomfortable with questions that allude to emotions. Since it is the facts of the loss that are often foremost in the bereaved's mind during early grief, the four-step process begins here.

Mourners may not be able to cope with the broader picture for a great while, but stating and restating facts is something those in the first stages of grief can handle and process with success. A gentle and nonintrusive inquiry into the specifics of who, what, when, where, and how is a natural and appropriate way to begin (e.g., "Can you tell me about the death?" "Where were you when it happened?" "How did you find out?").

Once they feel comfortable speaking, you will find that the bereaved are likely to tell and retell the story, linger over memories, and seem preoccupied with details. This is perfectly natural. Conversation centered around facts seems less invasive and threatening, requires less trust, and helps set the loss in a realistic perspective.

2. *Inquire about thoughts.* This sphere of questioning follows naturally from the sharing of facts by the bereaved. There are three areas you might explore:

- *first thoughts*—"My God, what did you think when you first heard?"
- *current thoughts*—"What have you been thinking about these days?"
- *repetitive thoughts*—"Is there a thought that you just can't get out of your mind?" "Do you find yourself thinking about some things over and over again?"

3. *Acknowledge and validate feelings.* After you have listened to the facts and some thoughts, perhaps several times, the bereaved is likely to recognize your interest and acceptance of their vulnerable state. At this point they may start talking spontaneously about their feelings. If they don't, you might ask the bereaved about them. One area for inquiry involves

feelings about the incident such as "How did you feel about the way you were told?" or "How did you feel about the memorial service?" Another area relates to feelings in the present such as "How do you feel now?" "How do you feel about receiving company today?" A third area addresses feelings about the bereaved's relationship with the deceased. Here you might ask something like "What did it feel like when you two first met?"

Don't be surprised if those in grief first discuss their feelings of fear, loneliness, anger, anxiety, and frustration. Love, tenderness, and feelings of nostalgia often come later, after the early anguish recedes.

A word of caution: Those in grief often feel very unstable and may be concerned about their hold on reality. While they may want to share these disquieting experiences, their ego, self-esteem, and need to "be strong" in front of others may pose a barrier to the free expression of perceptions, feelings, and experiences they think are unusual or abnormal. Examples of these natural but sometimes frightening experiences include hallucinations, fears of going "crazy," the desire for revenge, difficulty making decisions, anger toward the deceased, guilt over unresolved issues in the relationship, and anxiety over cruel words or perceived failures (see Chapter 2 for a discussion of the normal grief response). Such feelings are usually more readily expressed after the bereaved has seen that you are patient, ready to listen, nonjudgmental, and fully accepting.

4. *Reassure and support.* This phase of the conversation validates the bereaved's grief. As we have noted earlier, although many in grief question the normalcy of their feelings, most intense emotional grief reactions are healthy and natural expressions of the pain of loss. Typically, the bereaved will welcome sensitive reassurances that their feelings are normal and that they are not "losing touch with reality." Keep in mind that significant repetition may be required for your reassurances to be "heard."

Depending on the condoler's understanding of the grief

process, this phase may also involve talking with the bereaved about the stages of grief. Even the most general understanding of these stages can provide considerable support and will reassure the bereaved of the integrity and naturalness of their experience.

Remember that this chapter is about suggestions, not rigid rules. The ideas are presented to help you find your own way of listening to and conversing with someone in grief. Your personal style will evolve. Each time you reach out to another in need you learn, and that learning influences your next reaching.

Part V

What Can I Do?

We have much more to offer than we may realize. All we have to do is ask "How can I help?" with an open heart, and then really listen.

—Ram Dass and Paul Gorman, *How Can I Help?*

Chapter 13

Actions from the Heart

It's the most common expression of sympathy: "I'm so sorry. Is there anything I can do?" Yet these simple, heartfelt words frequently cast the bereaved into a dilemma. Those in the initial stages of grief scarcely hear the well-intentioned "What can I do?" let alone have the courage or clarity to respond with specific requests. Too often it seems there's a gap between condoling friends and the bereaved. Those who sincerely wish to help wonder what they can do, but don't know where to begin.

•

It was one of those lazy Sunday mornings. Bill had taken the kids fishing for the weekend and I had just curled up with a fresh cup of coffee and a magazine I'd been trying to get to for weeks. Just as the sun swung round to my easy chair, the ringing of the phone shattered the stillness. Hesitating for a moment, I decided to answer.

It was my friend, Maggie, sobbing. She quickly related that Ruben, the husband of Ellen, a close mutual friend, had been killed that morning in an automobile accident.

"The kids are at Sunday school and I am on my way to pick them up—can you drive over to Ellen's? She just heard the news."

I hesitated. My heart was bleeding for Ellen, but I was confused. "Of course, I'm on my way." I choked, "What should I do?"

There was a long silence. "I don't know; just be there. I'll join you as soon as I can."

As I grabbed a coat and my keys, my hands were shaking. Only two days before we'd gone to a movie with Ellen and

Ruben. He and Bill had talked about a hunting trip the following October. What could I possibly do to help at a time like this?

THE FIRST FEW HOURS

In the first few hours following a death, the thing to do if at all possible is to *be there.* Of course, this suggestion applies, in most cases, only to close friends and relations. If you are less familiar with the bereaved but feel moved to be with them, call. You may or may not be speaking directly with the bereaved since someone may already be assisting them by answering the phone. In any case, identify yourself clearly, explain that you have heard the news, and briefly express your sympathy and your wish to come over. Be direct in your request, without hesitation or ambivalence.

If the party answering is not the bereaved, and suggests that you not come over, you have several choices. You may follow the request, suggest coming later in the day (when others may have had to leave to tend to their affairs), or ask to talk to someone else. You may also ask to speak with the bereaved. They will have made it clear whether or not they wish to take such calls. Remember, yours may be one of many calls. It is considerate to be brief at this time.

If physical distance or particular circumstances prevent your going to them, you can still be of immense support. A poignant example was told by a middle-aged man whose wife suddenly died of a heart attack. He phoned his brother across the state to tell him the news. "Let me call your friends and the rest of the family" was the response. Within the hour, the grieving man found his two best friends at the front door.

If you are able to be physically present, don't be surprised when the bereaved later remembers little of what occurred in those first agonizing hours. The details may be vague, but those in grief typically recall with real gratitude the comforting presence of friends and genuine displays of warmth and caring:

That first morning was a blur and I guess I'm grateful that I can't recall very much about it. But the feeling of good people around me and the hugs . . . oh, God, I don't know how I would have made it without all those loving gestures.

Life is changed forever from the moment people are told about the death of a loved one. They feel helpless, powerless to control the events of their life. At the same time, they are swept up in a rapid tide of activity and the need for decisions, decisions, decisions: notifying relatives and friends, making funeral arrangements, taking care of newspaper notices, death certificates, phone calls, legal issues, financial and insurance matters, and a myriad of other details.

This demand to meet responsibilities can also be a blessing. In one sense these activities represent a final tribute to a loved one. They also help lift the veil of denial and disbelief and may act as a stabilizing influence. As the condoler, you must maintain a sensitive balance between providing assistance and understanding that when those who are bereaved carry out tasks, they are more open to the grief process.

There are so many ways you can be of service. If you plan to assist the bereaved in making funeral or memorial service arrangements, refer to the next chapter, Rites of Passage, Rites of Death. Other areas in which your help may be appreciated include the following:

- Phone calls need to be made to relatives and friends, clergy, the bereaved's physician, a funeral director, the bereaved's place of work, attorney, and so forth. You may offer to make the calls or just dial the numbers for the bereaved. In either case, keep a careful record of all calls near the phone.
- Put on a pot of tea or coffee or arrange for cold drinks both for the bereaved and for others who may be coming over shortly. Check the refrigerator to see that there's adequate food.
- If the bereaved needs to travel because the death occurred elsewhere, volunteer to make travel arrangements, help

pack, drive the bereaved to the airport, house-sit, clean out the refrigerator, take care of pets and plants, and collect mail. You may ask if anything needs to be canceled such as the newspaper or previously scheduled appointments.

Don't do anything that makes you uncomfortable or that you're clear will make the bereaved uncomfortable and don't offer more than you are prepared to give. Let the grieving persons know that you care, that you respect their wishes, and that—although you don't want to impose—you are ready and available to help.

IN THE DAYS THAT FOLLOW

During the next few days, repeated visits from close friends will be appreciated. The bereaved is unlikely to call you and ask you to come over. Don't wait for an invitation. Continue to be available as you are able. The bereaved is most likely to respond positively to specific offers such as "I'll wash the dishes," or "Why don't I get the phone for a while," always with a spoken or unspoken, "Is that okay?" Of course, another possibility is just to do something without asking, like bringing over food.

Before you jump in to help a bereaved friend, reflect for a few moments. Be aware and be sensitive and allow the bereaved to say no if what you're offering is perceived as an intrusion or simply is not wanted. Responding to the inner voice that says "I want to do something," keep in mind the following:

- *Consider the probable wishes and/or needs of the bereaved.* This chapter offers many suggestions that bereaved persons have shared with us as meaningful and helpful. You may want to consult with one of the bereaved's close friends or relatives for other ideas.
- *Select two or three gifts and/or services you can commit yourself to providing.*

- *If you've selected a gift such as bringing food or a book, just do it.* Include a note that lets the bereaved know from whom the gift came.
- *If you're willing to perform a practical service, make your offer something specific.* For example, you might suggest washing the car or picking up the drycleaning. Many more examples follow.
- *If you wish to spend time with the bereaved, consider asking to participate in an activity with him.* Again, ask the bereaved so that you do not intrude. For example, you might offer to go shopping with the bereaved or clean the house together. Listen and watch for clues that will help you respond to his needs, not yours.

Whatever your gift or offer, don't take a refusal or rejection personally. Make other offers at other times, even the next day. But do offer, do respond, do reach out. The biggest mistake is not making a wrong offer but withdrawing in fear of making a mistake or imposing with your simple expression of caring.

THOUGHTFUL GIFTS TO GIVE

Flowers, a traditional offering to the bereaved throughout the world, symbolize the beauty and the ephemeral quality of life. A friend once told us that during his sister's memorial service he heard little of what was being said but focused on a single white rose at the heart of a bouquet:

> It seemed to open as I watched; it was uncanny. It may sound strange, but I felt that it was her spirit opening to existence. I don't think I'd ever experienced the beauty of nature so intensely before or ever felt so much a part of it. I was overwhelmed with gratitude for that single blossom.

While floral tributes may represent love for the deceased, life's beauty, or happiness shared, for others cut flowers seem an extravagance, even a waste. A contribution to have a tree planted in honor of the deceased can be a beautiful alternative to sending fresh flowers. The gift of a sapling or a plant is also thoughtful and may be appreciated even more than flowers. Still another gift is the planting of a tree or plant in your own yard as a remembrance and writing a note to the bereaved telling of your thoughts and action. If the bereaved specifically requests charitable contributions in lieu of flowers, that request should be honored.

A young widow related how she treasured a flowering pot of chrysanthemums sent by a friend following the funeral. She found herself meticulously and lovingly tending to the plant and felt the life in the plant akin to her own. When the plant had a second blooming the following year, she saw it as a message supporting her in going forward with her own life. "I felt it bloomed just for me—no, I know it bloomed for me—it spoke through the opening of its blossoms and I needed to listen."

According to both the bereaved and funeral directors we have interviewed in the United States and Europe, regional and cultural preferences regarding floral tributes vary considerably. In France, for example, silk and other artificial flowers are preferred by many for their beauty, longevity, and absence of fragrance. Yet, in Holland, where fresh flowers are a major industry, artificial flowers are considered inappropriate. In the United States both are acceptable. If in doubt, send fresh flowers.

Bringing food to the bereaved is an ancient tradition. It has a universal quality that cuts across ethnic, religious, and social boundaries. Food is a symbol of sharing—it is a time-honored way of saying I want to help nurture you in some way during this most difficult time.

Keep in mind that the grieving family probably isn't eating regularly. Preparing or buying food and taking it to the home is most always appreciated. Sweets, special treats, or cold cut trays help feed visitors. Main dishes, salads, and fresh fruit save the family from having to cook. A young man related:

When my best friend's mother died, I brought over enough dinner for about eight people. Nothing fancy, just barbecued chicken and some salads. She said it was the best thing since there wasn't any real food for her family to eat. The cold cuts and stuff were pretty unappetizing by dinnertime and nobody felt like cooking.

If you're planning to do it on your own, or have joined with friends to prepare a complete meal for the family, let the bereaved know when it is coming. Label dishes on the bottom with the preparer's name on a piece of masking tape. We've heard from a number of bereaved who have been dismayed to take out a beautifully prepared dish from their refrigerator only to find that they didn't know whom to thank.

Of course, you do not have to supply a gourmet meal; a single dish or batch of cookies will be much appreciated. Just consider how you wish to express yourself. Since the bereaved may not use the item right away, it's thoughtful to wrap freezable dishes appropriately, labeling each with the name of the dish, date, instructions for preparation if appropriate, and name of donor. In a situation with many paying their respects, it is often helpful if someone volunteers to coordinate food gifts.

It is not a requirement that you give prepared food; bringing groceries can be a wonderful gift. You may also ask to do the grocery shopping for the bereaved or offer to take them shopping. Don't underestimate the importance of such simple gestures. Providing food is always a beautiful statement of caring and wanting to help. Do it more than once.

Giving a book is another thoughtful gesture. The most useful book may be one on coping with grief. There are many available for both adults and children. See the list of recommended books beginning on page 245. Other possibilities include photo essays, books of inspiration appropriate to the bereaved's beliefs, the sacred text of their religion such as the Bible or Koran, or collections of poetry. Another idea that is well received is a beautiful blank book or journal in which the bereaved may record their thoughts and feelings or whatever they like. You may choose to inscribe any gift book with a message of sympathy.

Creativity in gift giving has the potential to make a unique and thoughtful statement. A widower talked about appreciating a bottle of sherry from a good friend who told him, "I thought a little wine might help you have a gentler sleep some evenings." One condoler sent his own silver pen and a blank book. Another gave a sheet of "love" stamps and a box of blank thank-you note cards. An elderly widow said she most appreciated the electric blanket her sister sent. The friends of a researcher who died at his desk donated a rare book in his name to the college library. His parents received notes from both their son's friends and the library. A widower with three young children received a combined present from several of his wife's friends: a gift certificate for house-cleaning services. Other creative and appreciated gifts have included music boxes, art objects, recordings of music, and even a gift certificate for a massage.

Many of these suggestions may be adapted by those condolers who live far away. Flowers may be sent using wire services. We know of one person who sent a bouquet of daisies, the bereaved's favorite, once a week for six weeks. Other gifts, including books, music tapes or discs, or religious objects can be mailed with a note. Mail-order companies now feature a variety of appealing foods that make a thoughtful gift, but don't discount a "care package" of homemade baked goods lovingly wrapped and sent off in a bright tin box.

ACTS OF SERVICE

Another kind of gift is an act of service, no matter how small. A touching example was recounted to us by the bereaved mother of a teenage girl who had been killed in a camping accident. Lily's three closest girlfriends came by a couple of days after the funeral with a proposal. They wanted to come once a week for the next three months to help with the cleaning and other chores that had been Lily's.

I thought it might be difficult, but those visits were the highlight of my week. As we worked together, we chatted about school, boys, parents and, naturally enough, Lily. The spontaneity of those girls and their willingness to share both their grief over Lily's loss and their fond remembrances strengthened my days.

The following notes touch on a number of areas you might consider when thinking about activities or services to perform for the bereaved. You won't be alone in this desire to help. One of the ways you may assist is to remind other friends of the bereaved of ways in which they can participate. You may even want to coordinate a series of activities, acting as a liaison with the bereaved.

- Accompany the bereaved
  - to the funeral home
  - to the cemetery
  - on professional visits (lawyer, physician, accountant)
  - shopping
  - on miscellaneous errands
- Make phone calls to
  - relatives and friends
  - lawyer, physician, accountant
  - funeral director
  - bank or credit union
  - place of employment
  - social security office
  - child's school
  - insurance agent
- House-sit
  - during the funeral
  - if the survivor needs to leave town
- Help with the car and transportation; for example,
  - act as chauffeur
  - help out-of-town guests get to the funeral
  - transport children to school and activities
  - wash the car or fill it with gas
  - take in the car for servicing if needed

- Help with clothing by
  - taking care of laundry at your home or theirs
  - delivering and picking up dry cleaning
  - polishing shoes
  - loaning clothes if needed for funeral
- Help with pets by
  - overseeing feeding, care, and exercise
  - taking them to the veterinarian
  - buying pet food
- Care for the yard, for example,
  - mow the lawn
  - water plants
- Help with writing tasks such as
  - answering correspondence, including letters of condolence, maintaining a list of who phoned, who wrote condolence notes, who brought gifts
- Help with the bereaved's children by
  - offering to baby-sit
  - providing school transportation
  - helping with homework
  - taking the child with you when you shop for groceries
  - offering to take the child with your family to a movie, the library, park, or on other outings
  - reading a story
  - bringing (with parental permission) a book that helps children to understand death and grief (see the recommended list for children in the Suggested Readings)

DISPOSITION OF PERSONAL EFFECTS

Some bereaved are able to deal with the disposition of the deceased's personal effects several weeks after the death; others find the task extremely difficult and may take several months. A few others may keep the majority of personal effects for a prolonged period, even years. Let's look first at a misconception concerning this last group of individuals.

Just because the bereaved keep most personal effects for a prolonged period, doesn't necessarily mean they are experiencing abnormal grief. One mother, who apparently had a normal grief reaction, said that she closed the door to her deceased ten-year-old daughter's room for three years, disturbing nothing. "Then, one day I was just ready. I knew it had to be done, and with my husband's help, we went through Becca's things. There were tears, but it was manageable."

If, however, intense or persistent symptoms accompany this particular behavior, your bereaved friend or loved one may need help to move beyond grief. For a discussion of the key signs of abnormal grief, see Chapter 18, If Grief Is Too Much.

Far more typically, the bereaved will hold on to a few items that have special meaning: the clothing their loved one last wore, a special gift, a favorite object of art, books, or other mementos. Wallets and watches seem to be among the most frequently retained items by widows.

The disposition of remaining personal effects is an emotion-charged task that some bereaved unequivocally wish to do alone. Others will be grateful for the assistance of a close friend or relative.

If your offer to help is accepted, here is an approach that many with whom we have worked have found useful. Help the bereaved divide the deceased's belongings into three categories: (1) those that the bereaved clearly wishes to keep, (2) those they are fully prepared to give away, and (3) those items about which they are unsure.

This third category should be set aside for a few days or weeks, and then the process should be repeated with only these items. This process may take several sortings. It is imperative that you let the bereaved take the lead with each decision.

Trust the bereaved's cues. If they suddenly change their mind and cannot or do not wish to continue, honor that decision. And encourage talk while you're going through things. Don't be afraid to say, "Oh, I remember this. . . ." This is a time when a natural and healthy rekindling of sorrow often occurs.

Many bereaved wish to donate items to a charitable organization. You might offer to deliver the donation and pick up a receipt or to accompany the bereaved. The final letting go is often an emotional time.

EXTENDING INVITATIONS

Extend an invitation. How do you help guide your friend or loved one back into the world? Extending invitations is one of the first steps. An invitation after the acute phase of grief has begun to subside can give the bereaved their first encouragement, something to look forward to instead of feeling cut off or totally preoccupied with their grief. However, it is important to be aware that during bereavement it is rarely easy to reenter normal social interaction.

Bereaved people often decline invitations or accept only to cancel at the last minute. Hesitation or refusal is usually based on three unspoken factors. Either they are afraid of being rejected by others, are concerned about losing control of their emotions in public, or feel uncomfortable, even guilty, about doing something enjoyable or sociable.

- The mother of a son who committed suicide finally accepts an offer to shop for groceries with a friend. She feels shunned when, in the supermarket, a neighbor sees her but doesn't stop to say hello.
- A friend of a widower takes him to the movies and the bereaved man starts crying during a tender love scene. The friend says, "That's okay," holds the widower's arm for a moment, and adds, "There's no need to leave. I'm right here with you."
- Declining the lunch invitation of a business colleague, a widow says, "Go with someone else; you don't need to have lunch with a sad person."

The bereaved's concerns about rejection in public are not without foundation. But the cause is more likely to be that friends feel awkward and are concerned more about their own discomfort than reaching out to another in need. It also is true that the bereaved may become unpredictably emotional in public and this, particularly for those usually in control, can be very embarrassing. Your full acceptance of these emotional moments can set a healthy and healing example.

When extending an invitation, consider what the person has previously enjoyed doing. Does he or she like to go to the movies, the theater, museums? Take a drive to the seashore or mountains? Go out for lunch or dinner? You might invite the bereaved to your home for a casual meal. Again, remember shopping for groceries, clothes, or other basic items. Your invitation doesn't have to be for a special event.

Although invitations are often initially refused, they are typically much appreciated and convey a positive message to the bereaved. Be aware of and sensitive to the courage it may take for the bereaved to go out in public. Don't take a refusal personally; don't push too hard; don't neglect to ask again.

A friend or family member in grief may be beautifully responsive to your joining in an activity in which he or she is already engaged, such as cleaning the yard or washing dishes. Sometimes asking to join in a previously pleasurable activity can be extremely meaningful. There is a beautifully illustrative story recounted by the American spiritual teacher, Ram Dass, in his book, *The Only Dance There Is.* Upon the death of his mother, Ram Dass returned from India. On the drive home from the airport, his father spoke about how his own life was over, how his health was failing, how his only thoughts were dark ones.

Ram Dass made a conscious decision not to argue with his father about these feelings. Instead, when they arrived home, he asked to be shown how to make raspberry jam, a hobby of his father's. Working together, the two men sorted the berries, boiled them, and sterilized the jars. By the time the jam was set out to cool, his father's spirits were lighter and easier. As we discussed earlier, grief and sorrow are not feelings that you talk people out of, but by being authentically present with them, a healing and transforming change begins to happen. In the first days or weeks following a death, there may be many friends and relations striving to do just as you are doing. But often there is an abrupt decrease in support after the first two to four weeks. As a result, the bereaved may feel most isolated just when the intense pain of the loss begins to be most strongly experienced. One widower reported:

> I felt so alone after the first few days following Marge's death. I had thought the enormous support of friends and sympathetic neighbors would never stop. I was so grateful. Suddenly, the phone stopped ringing. No one came to visit anymore and I didn't know what to do. I thought maybe I had done something wrong. Those next few months were the loneliest in my life. I'll never let a friend in grief drift that way.

The importance of continued intermittent contact over the next few months, whether via notes, invitations, phone calls, visits, or offers to help with practical matters, cannot be overemphasized.

AFTERSHOCKS OVER THE YEARS

In the play, *I Never Sang for My Father,* Robert Anderson writes, "Death ends a life, but it does not end the relationship, which struggles in the survivor's mind towards some final resolution, some clear meaning, which it perhaps never finds." Acute grief comes to an end, but its aftermath echoes through the years. As time passes the bereaved will, on occasion, find poignant memories and feelings rekindled. Such feelings are often prompted by the anniversary of the death.

An anniversary, by definition, is the recurrence of an event or the reawakening of feelings surrounding an event that took place in the past. As the anniversary of joyous occasions prompt joyous memories, the anniversary of a loved one's death often stimulates feelings of grief and pangs of longing. On the anniversary of the death of King Albert of England, his daughter, Princess Alice, wrote the following letter to her mother, Queen Victoria:

Darmstadt,
December 11, 1866

Beloved, precious Mama,

On awakening this morning, my first thoughts were of you and of dear darling Papa! Oh, how it reopens the wounds scarcely healed, when this day of pain and anguish returns! This season of the year, the leafless trees, the cold light, everything reminds me of that time!

Happily married as I am, and with such a good, excellent and loving husband, how far more can I understand now the depth of that grief which tore your lives asunder!

The first anniversary, holiday, or special occasion after a death often rekindles an intense return of grief. Just as the bereaved is beginning to feel adjusted to a life without their loved one, these anniversary reactions can stimulate profound fears that they are slipping back into the anguish of their earlier grief.

On the date of their wedding anniversary, a widower whose wife died the year before found himself "suddenly drowning" in grief. "I thought I'd been doing quite well since Edna's death. I'd returned to my job, renewed interest in old hobbies and had recently begun to do a little socializing with close friends."

One morning, after a fitful night's sleep, he awoke feeling depressed and uneasy. When he arrived at work and saw the date on his calendar, he realized the cause. "I started crying right there at my desk. It would have been our thirty-sixth wedding anniversary. Realizing what had triggered it didn't help. I found myself at the edge of panic with the idea that the pain of grief might be starting all over again. It was terrifying."

Similar responses may be fostered by times of celebration or tender moments the survivor would like to have shared with the deceased.

- A sudden flood of tears surprises a bride because her father, dead for many years, is not there to walk her down the aisle.

- A mother is overcome with sadness while watching spectacular fireworks on the Fourth of July as she remembers how much her young son, who died three years previously, delighted in the magic of these displays.
- A father, during the baptism of his third son, finds himself catapulted into grief by the memory of his first and stillborn child several years before.
- A widow who had long dreamt of a trip to Spain with her husband makes the trip alone five years after his death. Although she has been eagerly anticipating the holiday, when disembarking from the plane she finds herself inexplicably depressed, confused over her feelings, and longing for her husband.

Such responses are not only triggered by the anniversary of a death or special occasions. Pain, spontaneous tears, and deep feelings of sadness surface at unexpected times and in unexpected places. These aftershocks of grief, whether they are embarrassing or comforting, rejected or welcome, are important reminders of what the relationship has meant. These moments may come about while driving, listening to certain music, or participating in specific activities like shopping for a special food, going for a walk, watching a movie, or playing a game. Sometimes the association between the activity or situation and the triggering of the momentary return of grief is clear; other times it is a puzzle known only to the unconscious.

Condolers can provide immense relief by helping the bereaved to understand that these aftershocks are not setbacks or an indication of unresolved grief. Such responses are natural, cleansing, and can be intense loving reminders of relationships now past. They may be surprising, but need not be devastating.

Frequently friends and loved ones of the bereaved avoid mentioning the deceased on anniversaries and other special occasions. They imagine that the bereaved will only feel badly or depressed by such a reminder. Over and over, the bereaved have told us that the opposite is true; they are hurt by the avoidance. As a group, those whose loved ones have died deeply appreciate and cherish acknowledgment of the death on anniversaries, birthdays, and other special occasions. This message may be given in direct conversation, by phone or in a note or card.

We've heard many accounts of such simple and thoughtful gestures. For example, one widow told us of the pleasure she received when a good friend sent her a note on what would have been the widow's twentieth wedding anniversary.

> I know that you and Jack would have been celebrating your twentieth anniversary this week and wanted to tell you that I've been thinking about the love you two shared. Hope all is well; I'll call you later this week.

A second example was told to us: A friend of a graduating high school senior approached her after the ceremony with congratulations and added that she, too, missed the graduate's mother who had died the year before. The graduate told us, "I was so aware that Mom wasn't there; I'd been aware all year that she wouldn't be and it hurt awfully. When Cindy came over to me and talked about my Mom I realized that someone else missed her, too. It meant as much as my graduation."

When you acknowledge these times of remembrance, the bereaved may respond with sadness. But to interpret this as a negative response or a reason to avoid such action is to miss the point. Your expression of tender understanding at a time of obvious remembrance is almost always received as a gift from the heart.

Chapter 14

Rites of Passage, Rites of Death

If we give our heart's attention to the rituals we need, we can create the sacred time and space in which to say good-bye to a loved one. Through ritual, we create a sacred circle in which to let our love as well as our tears flow.

—JUDITH SARA SCHMIDT, *HOW TO COPE WITH GRIEF*

In the immediate aftermath of a death, some bereaved may be confused and nearly paralyzed with grief whereas others, equally pained by the loss, may function with remarkable efficiency and apparent ease. For some, in a world that seems to have gone out of control, this time of decision making provides a stabilizing influence and a feeling of mission that is very important. For others, the situation is one of only painful decisions. In *Grief: The Mourning After,* Catherine Sanders, Ph.D., reports in her studies of bereaved spouses that making arrangements at the funeral home was considered difficult for all of them. "Generally, the surviving spouse was accompanied by grown children, relatives, or friends who helped in the selection of various alternatives concerning the ritual itself" (p. 189).

If you are willing and close enough to the bereaved, both physically and in the nature of your relationship, your assistance in these often painful matters can be invaluable. If you are not close enough to feel comfortable taking a primary role in this area but are willing to help, you might consider calling those who are functioning in this way to offer your help in peripheral activities. Some of these are listed in Chapter 13, Actions from the Heart.

HOW WE SAY GOOD-BYE

In all condoling actions, it is important to reflect on your own experiences of and attitudes toward loss. But more than that, many who have been active in condoling also find it helpful to reflect on society's attitudes toward death. Few people are comfortable with the word *funeral* let alone the fact. For one who wishes to assist a close bereaved friend or loved one during this period, this chapter offers an overview of issues surrounding the rites of death.

Confronting another's death unavoidably reminds us of our own mortality, so society has created a variety of methods to minimize direct confrontation with another's passing. Despite the recent surge of frankness about dying, our culture continues to be uncomfortable with the finality of death. Upon visiting America, the great French writer, Albert Camus, called us "this country where everything is done to prove that life isn't tragic." Attention to the subject of death is often considered morbid and unnatural and its intrusions leave many of us at a loss for a suitable response. As a result, we isolate the aged in their own communities and then use euphemisms like "passed away" to explain their dying. We bar children from most hospital terminal wards and funerals. During the last fifty years in Western cultures, fewer and fewer children and young adults have participated in the death rituals of another person. Such distancing is unfortunate. Death rites serve four major and critical purposes:

- To memorialize the deceased.
- To reinforce for the bereaved a network of caring relationships.
- To comfort those in grief.
- To bring to the bereaved a realistic awareness of the finality of the loss.

Funerals and other rites of passage have a way of defining who we are and what things mean. When families and friends come together to celebrate births, baptisms, bar mitzvahs, graduations, weddings, and anniversaries, these are times of reunion. Funerals and memorial services also represent times of reunion and renewal for relationships. Participation in these rituals involves an active process of association that helps many to clarify feelings, relationships, and beliefs.

The customs that are associated with the death of a loved one can be an important catalyst in the healing journey. For many, participation in these rites marks a turning point, a time when the numbness and detachment fade and the bereaved is confronted by the anguish of loss in a world that seems all too real. It is a time when condoling friends can be of particular support.

As important as they are, don't be surprised if a grieving friend later recalls little of these rituals, including your supporting presence. Although some bereaved recollect these events with great clarity, others have difficulty remembering at all. Still others create an idealized and poetic vision filtered through their loving experiences with the deceased as in the poem "The Funeral," by Gordon Parks. In this poem the narrator returns to the town of his youth for his father's funeral. Through adult eyes everything appears to be much smaller than it did when he was a boy. But there is one exception: "Only the giant who was my father / remained the same. / A hundred strong men strained beneath his coffin / When they bore him to his grave."

DIFFICULT CHOICES

The death of a loved one requires that the bereaved make many choices at a time when their minds may not be clear. Those in grief and funeral directors alike have told us how helpful it can be to have a friend or relative with the bereaved when decisions regarding final plans for the deceased are made. A caring yet somewhat detached companion can provide solid support and clarity in the face of the need to make these emotionally charged choices. The bereaved will have to arrange for a memorial service or funeral, choose a casket or urn, provide information for a death notice, select pall bearers, choose an officiant, choose music and flowers, prepare the home for visitors, and make numerous other decisions.

Of course, not everyone elects to hold a service for the deceased. Funeral directors we have interviewed point out that 15 percent to 25 percent of families choose to have no funeral or memorial service at all. The reasons are many. Great distances may separate loved ones. Families are often no longer neatly defined as nuclear units, sometimes making the question of who to inform and invite an awkward one. The deceased may have lived in a community where he or she was not known well. For some bereaved, ambivalent or antagonistic feelings toward the deceased may cause them to reject the idea of a funeral. Still other belief systems recognize no need to "honor" the body of the deceased.

Even when such practical considerations are not a factor, the bereaved may simply wish to avoid a public marking of the death. Of course, as one funeral director put it, "Not having a funeral does not mean not having grief." As a condoler, your role is simply to support the bereaved's decision. Not to persuade, just to support.

Initially, and depending on your closeness to the bereaved, you can help by offering to be with them throughout all or part of the planning stage and by being available to do the following:

1. Contact a funeral director. This is a trained professional who is familiar with procedures and can assist in many areas immediately following the death. One funeral director put it aptly: "My job is to help the family do what they want to do, to remove detail from their shoulders so that they can focus on their own priorities such as what to wear to the funeral and who to invite."
2. Contact the cemetery. This may be done by the funeral director.

3. Support and assist in selection of the type of service and its time and place.
4. Support the bereaved's wishes regarding selection of a casket, flowers, grave marker, pall bearers, and so on. This is a delicate area for many because the bereaved may be inclined to spend more money on these final arrangements than is prudent considering their financial situation. The average price of a funeral in the United States exceeds $3,800. If you are close enough to the bereaved to be aware of such circumstances, gently make your suggestions; then be prepared to uphold their final choices.
5. Offer to help choose what the bereaved will wear to the funeral or memorial service.
6. Offer to notify friends, relatives, and business colleagues. If it isn't a function of the funeral director, call the local newspaper for placement of a funeral notice and obituary.
7. Help consider the question of whether or not children should attend. If they do, you may offer to sit with them during the service to help them understand what is going on and provide open support for them to express their feelings.
8. Contact a member of the clergy or spiritual officiant, if any.
9. Help the bereaved decide whether they prefer condolers to send floral tributes, make charitable contributions in the name of the deceased, or do something else.

Along with funeral arrangements, many financial and legal decisions must be made by the bereaved in the period immediately following a death. It seems ironic that such important matters demand attention at a time when the bereaved may feel least able to make well-thought-out choices. Although the legal advice of friends and family is usually well-intended, this advice may be less than objective and may be based on limited expertise. In our experience, the practical and emotional support of family and close friends combined with the competent advice of professionals is invaluable. Condolers may assist in obtaining and completing paperwork, make phone calls, and do research. It's crucial that clear records of all contacts made on behalf of the bereaved be documented and explained carefully.

Of the many lists available to guide the bereaved in this area, one of the most useful is published by the Life Insurance Marketing and Research Association in a booklet entitled *What Do You Do Now?* Each item below is covered in greater detail in the booklet. It is available free of charge through most life insurance agents and life insurance companies. The following list is adapted from this publication and suggests specific ways in which you may help:

1. Obtain multiple, certified copies of the death certificate. These will be needed to notify banks and financial institutions, Veterans' Administration, life insurance and mortgage companies, stocks and bonds, unions, Social Security Administration, retirement funds, and so on.
2. Consult a lawyer.
3. Locate important papers.
4. Contact insurance agent or life insurance company.
5. Contact local Social Security Office.
6. If deceased was a civil service employee and bereaved meets requirements, apply for benefits.
7. If deceased was a veteran, contact the nearest Veterans' Administration Office for possible benefits.
8. Contact the deceased's employer and/or business associates.
9. Contact organizations to which the deceased belonged.
10. If appropriate, the bereaved may need to visit their trust officer.
11. Gather the deceased's current bills and notify creditors of the death.
12. Contact a tax expert if you believe the estate is subject to taxation.
13. Contact probate court and file will.
14. Call social services or welfare agencies if appropriate.

SPECIAL ISSUES

Many emotionally charged issues arise when confronting the choices that must be made following a death. The four areas that follow are the ones we've been asked about most frequently by condolers:

THE PRESENCE OF CHILDREN

In his book *Talking About Death: A Dialogue Between Parent and Child,* Earl Grollman writes:

> Just as your children cannot be spared knowledge about death, they cannot and should not be excluded from the grief and mourning following death. They too have both a right and a need to say good-bye. (p. 56)

Condolers are not infrequently asked their opinion about the appropriateness of children at funeral or memorial services. There are differing opinions regarding this issue among both professionals and parents, but the majority favor the involvement of children in these rites. While circumstances vary widely, we strongly support the position that children beyond the age of toddlers, who know well either the bereaved or the deceased, be involved in this experience. Rites should always be explained beforehand at a level commensurate with the child's ability to understand. If you have a close relationship with a bereaved child you might offer to read and discuss with the child one of the suggested books on grief or death listed in the Suggested Readings.

Even when parents wish to involve their children, they may hesitate for fear that they will be unable to attend to the children appropriately while enmeshed in their own grief. A caring friend or relative may ask the parents beforehand if they wish them to either take care of the children directly during the services, or be close by and assume responsibility if needed. Equanimity may be needed as children's expressions of grief, including anger and loud crying, should not be suppressed.

Children should always be asked if they wish to attend, perhaps be gently encouraged but never forced. Attendance at the service is not easy for a child, but as with adults, it is an important rite of passage during which the finality of death is acknowledged while expressions of caring and grieving are supported. It's an opportunity for the child to experience firsthand a unique sense of community. It is important that the child not be excluded from participating in the condoling activities that follow the service. For a more detailed discussion on the grief of children and adolescents, see pages 58–66 and 85–86.

Being with the Body

Sometimes a casket is left partially or fully open for the purpose of viewing the body. This is often the most difficult portion of the funeral rite for the bereaved and those who condole. But for many, it is an integral part of the ceremony and helps the bereaved to say good-bye, ask forgiveness, personally place treasured items in the casket, or offer a final caress to the deceased.

A remarkable scene is described in C. David Heymann's book *A Woman Named Jackie* (Signet, 1989), a biography of Jacqueline Kennedy. Following President Kennedy's assassination, his body was returned to the White House. Before burial, Jackie wished to place in the casket some small mementos and notes from the children. She asked Bobby Kennedy to accompany her to the East Room where they were met by Godfrey McHugh who was in charge of the Honor Guard. McHugh helped them open the coffin:

> She gazed at her husband's face. She began to stroke his hair and continued to caress it as the minutes ticked by. Sensing what she wanted, McHugh left the room and quickly returned with a pair of scissors. Jackie bent forward

and carefully cut a lock of the President's hair. Bobby slowly lowered the lid of the coffin. Jackie turned and left the room. (p. 424)

Seeing the body of their loved one assists many to confront the finality of the death, stimulates the release of feelings, and provides closure. For others, in accordance with some religious practices or in some cases of violent death, the casket may remain closed.

To sit silently in the presence of the body of a loved one who has recently died—for minutes or even several hours—is extremely important and meaningful for many people. This stems from both religious and ancient spiritual practices and appears to be increasing as a practice in Western culture. From a psychological as well as a spiritual point of view this final physical parting can touch deep feelings of separation and release. It provides time to say unsaid things and to rest in still moments of meditation or prayer. We have talked with many who wished they'd spent more time with their loved one in death.

Sitting with the body also provides a special opportunity to physically touch the deceased. In hospices throughout the United States and Europe, loved ones are strongly encouraged to spend at least some time with the body. In Paris, at the extraordinary hospice Unité de Soins Palliatif, we were touched to learn that a loved one may participate with the medical team in the traditional washing of the body after death. Physical contact may be difficult or even impossible for some, but many appreciate a final chance to gently kiss, caress, or hug their loved one. It is here that death, love, and sorrow meet.

If you are a close friend or relative, you can offer your opinion about spending time with the body of the deceased. You also might offer to accompany the bereaved to the viewing location either to sit with them or to wait outside until after their private moments.

Cremation

Cremation, the burning of a body to ashes, is an option increasingly chosen for a variety of reasons including substantial reduction in expense. It is important to recognize that cremation does not preclude viewing the body.

Before the cremation takes place, the bereaved will be asked about disposition of the ashes. Where they rest is a matter of personal preference and local law. In many areas the choices are confined to the bereaved's home, a designated cemetery, or over the ocean. Some choose to retain the ashes in their home in a traditional urn, while others select creative alternatives. We know of one bereaved woman who decided against a traditional urn in favor of her deceased grandmother's favorite cookie jar! This was a container always associated with warmth and tender memories and she knew that looking at it would make her smile.

Final Resting Place

Where the body rests can have particular significance for the bereaved. This is more important for some than for others, but having a place with which to identify the one now gone can be of great comfort. Even if the deceased has not been given a traditional earth burial in a cemetery, there are many ways of "marking" a spot. If the deceased has been cremated and the ashes dispersed, a grave marker may still be purchased for location in a cemetery. An adult son recounted how helpful this was after the death and cremation of his second parent: "I had a marker placed in a beautiful local cemetery commemorating my parents' lives. It wasn't for them as much as it was for me. It gave me a place to visit with them."

Creative alternatives to a grave site or marker include designating a favorite place or item of the deceased such as a viewpoint, park bench, tree, cherished personal possession, or particular piece of music:

> After we scattered the ashes, I felt lost for a time because there was no particular place to go like a cemetery. A lot of things reminded me of Jon, but I found I wanted something or some place specific. One afternoon I was looking at a sculpture of a dancer that Jon and I had bought and both loved. In my heart, I knew that was it. Since then, that little sculpture is the place I go whenever I need to connect with Jon. It works. I don't know how.

Such a choice as the one just described can provide the sense of being with the deceased that is, for many, so comforting. What is important is that whatever is selected as a personal memorial is designated and used as such.

Part VI

The Challenge to Our Beliefs

The world is not respectable; it is mortal, tormented, confused, deluded forever; but it is shot through with beauty, with love, with glints of courage and laughter; and in these, the spirit blooms timidly, and struggles to the light amid the thorns.

—George Santayana

Chapter 15

Why Me?

How do you answer when your bereaved friend suddenly looks up, gazes into your eyes, and asks "Why me?" The truth is that there are no simple answers, but there are helpful ways of responding.

When life is going smoothly in health, relationships, work, and play, we rarely ponder the question "Why me?" But life is a roller coaster and no one escapes the anguish of loss. The pain of adversity often triggers our most basic questioning about the meaning of life, our faith, and the presence of a higher spiritual being. In his book, *A Gift of Hope: How We Survive Our Tragedies,* Robert Veninga reflects:

> I kept asking: How do we survive the injustices that life puts in our path? How do we survive the loss of precious people? How do we cope when a terrifying diagnosis is given? And how can we ever believe in God—or in the goodness of life—when that which makes life so rich and beautiful is suddenly taken from us?

To grieve is to embark on a journey not of our own making. It is a journey that is both perilous and unpredictable. But grief also reminds us of the degree to which we have loved. It is an opportunity for self-analysis and an opening to our compassion for ourselves, the deceased, and others. Meaning arises in the form of insights, understanding, gratitude, appreciation of our limitations and, perhaps most importantly, acceptance of our not knowing all the answers. Ultimately, those who are willing to fully face the experience of their grief emerge from the loss with a strong sense of the preciousness of life. The sensitive condoler who empathizes with a friend in grief is also on a journey and condoling actions may provoke insights and appreciation for his or her own life.

The first, most obvious, and most charged question asked by those who believe in a personal God and by atheists alike is an inevitable response to suffering. "Why me?" is not only a question but a cry, not only an inquiry but an enigma. At the root of the Judaic-Christian culture is the notion that the world is fair—or at least ought to be fair. The plea, even the demand of the child within us, is that the world *should* be fair. As we mature we recognize that if the world is indeed fair, it is not by our understanding of "fairness." Yet, in suffering, our earlier pleas for "fairness" are reawakened. Hence the question, "Why me?" and the attached emotions of anger, disappointment, and confusion.

In his acclaimed best-seller, *When Bad Things Happen to Good People,* Harold S. Kushner writes:

> There is only one question that really matters: Why do bad things happen to good people? All other theological conversation is intellectually diverting . . . virtually every meaningful conversation I have ever had with people on the subject of God and religion has either started with this question or gotten around to it before long . . . they are all troubled by the unfair distribution of suffering in the world. (p. 6)

HOW TO RESPOND

To deal with the most basic question of "Why me?" you need to put aside the part of you that desires to fix things and give advice. Despite your good intentions, you cannot perform this function. Perhaps even more challenging, you must also put aside your own ache for rational explanations. What you *can* do is help to create an atmosphere in which healing may occur. This must be done while allowing the bereaved to experience their anguish and their questioning. Through this process, they may come to a new place inside themselves, altering their priorities and even their perception of the world. You can support this opportunity for them to be, to see, and to learn.

As in all conversations with the bereaved, begin by giving your total attention as you listen to the questions concerning "Why me?" Attempt to gain an accurate perception of their concerns and a sense of their anguish. This is one of the simplest, most meaningful, and compassionate gifts you can give. It is the process of *trying* to understand that has the impact and it is an unending process. Authentic questions will convey far more compassion than "perceptive" statements.

It is important to relate to the feelings behind the question "Why me?" Remember that the question is a cry, not an inquiry. Accept and support expressions of anger, disappointment, and sadness. You might say "How can you take it?" or "If this happened to me I'd be furious, too." Rabbi Pesach Krauss, in his book *Why Me?,* writes:

> That "Why me?" is sometimes shouted, "WHY ME?! Why did God do this to ME?" in such a way that I know the patient is beside himself with rage. Well, I never get into a theological discussion at that time because that's not what the patient is really seeking. Logic, at this point, will have little effect. It certainly will not be listened to. That comes later. First I have to deal with the emotions the patient is expressing. (pp. 44–45)

You may say "I don't know either why God has done this; you must feel terrible," or "This just doesn't make sense. It feels so unfair." Whatever your response, accept the bereaved's emotions, their pleas, and their demands that the world be different.

Being present and unconditionally accepting is an attitude, not a technique. It conveys that you care for and respect the mourner with a foundation that is unshakable, that you are not using this interaction to judge them or the quality of their love or their response to loss. Acceptance of the bereaved's religious or spiritual beliefs—or their doubting of such beliefs—is crucial.

Whether a person is an atheist, a spiritualist, a Buddhist, a Christian, or a Jew, this is not the time to impose your own beliefs. It is not the time to persuade someone to become a believer. Relate to the pain of the suffering person. You can bring the fragrance of a higher spiritual being by listening with an open heart, integrity, sincerity, and by dedicating your life to the moment. See yourself as relating soul to soul, not belief system to belief system. By listening in this manner you elevate the bereaved's self-worth, validate their life experience, and nourish their sense of dignity in the midst of agony. You may pray together, meditate together, or allow moments of precious silence. Whether the bereaved are finding solace through their faith or in turmoil, attempting to reconcile their faith with their sense of the grave injustice done to them or to their deceased loved one, your function remains the same: Be present, listen, accept, and support.

RELIGIOUS CONSOLATION

In the first stages of acute bereavement, those in grief rarely appreciate religious explanations or your coming to God's defense when they question, "Why me?"

No one understands or truly knows why any death occurs or can fully explain the timing of death from any cause. There's a wonderful little story of a disciple who approached his Zen master with a question:

> "What is death?" the disciple queried.
> His master smiled, "I do not know."
> "How can that be? You are a Zen master!"
> "That is true, but I am not a dead Zen master."

Attempting to provide explanations only interferes with the pain of loss for the bereaved and is almost always received with resistance, even anger. Such "answers" may cause the bereaved to run from spirituality as a safe harbor for understanding and courage.

In his book *A Grief Observed,* C. S. Lewis notes:

> Talk to me about the truth of religion and I'll listen gladly. Talk to me about the duty of religion and I'll listen submissively. But don't come talking to me about the consolations of religion or I shall suspect that you don't understand.

To try to make sense and find meaning is an unwavering quality of the human mind. However, one approach typically triggers anger or at least irritates, even when presented by those condolers who respond out of compassion. Be wary about such statements as "It was God's will," or declaring that the bereaved should "trust in the wisdom of the Lord," or that "God doesn't do anything without a purpose."

If you have a theology, belief system, or religion of your own that is different from the bereaved's, and you wish to share certain aspects with them, do so, *but cautiously.* Present your thoughts as an alternative, as a possibility. Do not try to tell a bereaved person what or how to believe. Personal faith is a highly charged issue and, no matter how well-meaning, proselytizing, especially at a time of grief, can be very offensive.

If you feel a need to do something more than be fully present as a listener, it may be helpful to acknowledge that "It is indeed true that of the many things about life and living we cannot explain, death is the most difficult to understand."

For those bereaved who have close ties to their religion or spiritual practice, consider ways to support that faith. This may be as simple as asking to accompany them to their place of worship, making a contribution to their church, temple, or religious charity in the name of their loved one, or letting them know you are remembering them in your meditations or prayers.

The following list includes a number of other ways through which you may show your respect and concern. If you're not sure where to begin, contact your own religious leader, local funeral director, or the yellow pages under Hospice.

- Encourage the bereaved to contact their spiritual leader and to be open about their feelings and questions.
- Contact a local grief or hospice group and ask for the names of clergy of the bereaved's denomination who have special training in grief counseling.
- Contact the national center of the bereaved's religious group and ask for literature or other material for those in grief.
- Obtain books written by people with a religious orientation in the direction of the bereaved's faith, such as those written by a rabbi, minister, or priest.
- Present as a gift for the bereaved a religious object such as a cross, meditation cushion, Bible, vajra, Star of David, or candle.

THE SHIFT FROM "WHY ME?" TO "WHAT NOW?"

Despite the easing over time of emotional storms associated with the question "Why me?" questioning continues. Subsequent questions are a window. They often reflect an increased realization that the most important questions about life are unanswerable, that our time on this earth is not a perplexity to be unraveled, but a mystery to be lived and hopefully appreciated.

Eventually, the question is transformed from "Why me?" to "What can I do now that my life has changed?" Through the healing process of grief, bereaved individuals slowly reorient their energies to the unfinished tasks of their life. This letting go of the question "Why me?" is usually associated with a shift in feelings away from the unrelenting surges of irrational anger that are so much a part of the initial phases of grief. Out of this, for most people, there emerges an increased appreciation of the ephemeral and cherished qualities of life.

As friends we cannot, nor should we, attempt to hurry the process. We can, however, through our sensitive presence and continued encouragement, provide support during this pivotal time.

Following the death of three friends, Michael Nesset poignantly expressed his own transformation of attitude in an article in *The Sun* magazine (issue 169):

> Three good people died in the middle of their lives and through no fault of their own, and I find myself asking why they died, and discovering that the answers that used to comfort me are suddenly out of date. . . . In the year that has passed since the first of these deaths, my philosophies have regained none of their old power to comfort and explain. The terrible truths have lost none of their power either—though the shock is gone—and my world will never be quite the same. Every meal with my family, every walk with my wife, every chance to untangle a paragraph or talk to a child or search for galaxies on a clear night—all have a sharper edge than before, a subtle urgency, an air of passing away that makes me want to take all the chances that come along, and keep my eyes and ears wide open and my mouth more often closed, so that I miss nothing. I have less time to waste on anger, or on the endless enterprises of being vindicated and being understood.

When we cope successfully with the pain of loss, transcending this most human of experiences, we gain a sense of perspective on life, a deeper appreciation of the human condition, and draw closer to the essence of love and compassion.

Chapter 16

A Spiritual Perspective

There are more things in heaven and earth, Horatio, than are dreamt of in your philosophy.

—*Hamlet,* Act I, sc. 5

THE TRANSCENDENT AND THE MYSTERIOUS

Mysticism is the experience that life is not logical, that life is more like poetry and music than like mathematics. Mysticism declares that life can never be fully known; it is essentially incomprehensible by ordinary standards.

Individuals in mourning often report experiences that fall into the realm of the mystical. Most of these reports involve receiving "messages" from their deceased loved one or experiencing unlikely coincidences surrounding the death. These uncanny events come in many forms: intense dream "visions," the blooming of a rare or long-awaited flower, dramatic changes in the weather, finding a meaningful lost object or letter, or other unusual occurrences.

Other reported phenomena include out-of-body experiences during which the bereaved can sometimes see their deceased loved one or even visit with them. Some report seeing or hearing Jesus, Moses, Mohammed, Buddha, or other beloved spiritual figures.

It is too easy to dismiss mystical incidents as figments of the imagination and to deny their possible connection with other realities. Of course, proof or verification is impossible in these realms of "seeing," but as condolers we must not be so presumptuous as to "know" that these experiences are unfounded. This attitude discredits both the bereaved and the encounter.

Those having such experiences are often firmly convinced of their reality. As a condoler, let your capacity for truth expand into uncharted waters and allow yourself to be in a state of simple acceptance. If you can listen without judgment, the bereaved will be more likely to share these precious and sometimes confusing experiences. In an article for *The Sun,* a "magazine of ideas" (issue 169, p. 39), entitled "The Man in the Mirror," Sy Safransky eloquently expressed his difficulty in staying with these powerful, transcendent, and potentially transforming events:

> I've known moments of transcendence—ecstatic experiences of oneness that have shown me, beyond any doubt, that death is nothing to fear. But, like distant islands in a vast sea, these moments can seem remote, inaccessible. Most of the time, I cling to this weathered lifeboat, this body, and don't like being reminded it wasn't built to last. . . . It's hard for me to embrace the paradox that I'm going to die and that who I really am never dies. . . . To acknowledge the fear, as well as the fearless essence of me, is no small task.

People often experience these transcendent moments as truths. Whether triggered by grief or not, such times rekindle a sense of wonder and make us take special note. These uncanny incidents, often far outside the realm of everyday life, are frequently associated with a powerful urge to share and a simultaneous fear of being misunderstood or negatively judged.

Susan, a thirty-one-year-old nurse, lost her husband in an auto accident. At her urging, he had stopped smoking just two weeks before his death. In her grief, she expressed her guilt about the discomfort and unhappiness he experienced as a result of his quitting smoking. A month after his death, Susan reported the following dream:

> I was walking along a path . . . I was at the edge of something vast . . . there was a point, a place I reached, beyond

which was darkness. . . . I couldn't see. . . . I was afraid to step into it. . . . I knew I was supposed to take that step . . . there was no turning back. . . . I summoned up all my courage and did it. . . . Suddenly . . . there was my husband bathed in light. Smiling, he said with that exquisite twinkle in his eyes, "Don't feel guilty about helping me to stop smoking; don't feel guilty about anything. Just remember our love." As I reached out for him, he blew me a kiss and then disappeared. I woke up sobbing, but something had lifted.

Ken Wilber wrote an extraordinary account of his wife's death from cancer that appeared in *The New Age Journal* (July/August 1989). In it, he vividly described the high winds associated with her dying.

> Treya closed her eyes, and, for all purposes, she never opened them again. . . . It was at that moment that I began to notice that the atmosphere had become very turbulent. . . . The wind began whipping up a ferocious storm; our ordinarily rock solid house was shaking and rattling in the gale-force winds . . . [later documented to be record-breaking winds]. The next morning, Treya settled into the position in which she would die. . . . Exactly five minutes after her death, the gale-force winds ceased blowing. [This, too, was noted in the next day's papers.]

Wilber continues:

> The ancients have a saying: "When a great soul dies, the winds go wild." The greater the soul, the greater the wind necessary to carry it away. A great, great soul had just died, and the wind responded.

In the realm of the transcendent and the mysterious, we must help the bereaved to remember and honor their dreams, their visions, and their experiences, however inexplicable. These events in grief may be among the most profound in humanity's unrelenting search for meaning and inspiration.

CRISIS AND OPPORTUNITY

A core loss catapults each of us into the void. Some close their eyes; others open them. Essentially, there are two paths of coping with the anguish that ensues. One is to tolerate the pain or strive to diminish it with denial, drugs, alcohol, and other means. Caring helpers may unwittingly support this path by making the "comfort" of the bereaved their first priority. The second path, the one "less traveled by," is to confront the pain and be open to the challenge of what has happened and is happening. This choice allows for the possibility of opening into a new way of being. A rebirth. Other cultures recognize this phenomenon in their very languages. The Hebrew word for crisis is *mashber,* and the same word refers to the travail of a woman in childbirth. The Chinese word for crisis consists of two small pictures or characters called ideograms. One means danger and the other opportunity. The ancient Chinese recognized that dangers are never without opportunity and opportunity does not exist without danger. It simply depends on one's perspective. A crisis of death often brings about new ways of living, seeing, and being. Throughout the centuries, sages have reminded us that learning how to accept death is critical to accepting, appreciating, and enjoying life.

In her book *The Ultimate Loss* (Beaufort Books, 1982), Joan Bordow reflects on the gap between our expectations and life as it is:

> Death affords those who are left an opportunity to re-evaluate everything. And though we would give all we have to defer that opportunity, it exists anyway. It allows us to see the flimsiness of our expectations, to realize there is not expectation without disappointment; it allows us the possibility to being more sensitive, more vulnerable, to let others support us, and to notice the integrity and love often left unobserved in life's fast pace. Mainly, it gives us the chance to live life in the present. (p. 19)

Through crisis come opportunities for continuing maturation and deepening compassion and actualization. The bereaved may enlarge their perspective, gaining wisdom and understanding. Again, remember that this is a process that takes time and cannot be forced. Although it's a phase of the journey that must be traveled by the bereaved alone, as one who condoles you can ease the way with patience, acceptance, and nonjudgment. For both the bereaved and the condoler the real opportunity, unwelcome as it may be in the moment, is for personal growth. Henry Wadsworth Longfellow recognized this when he said: "It has done me good to be somewhat parched by the heat and drenched by the rain of life."

Surprisingly enough, it is usually not one's attitude toward death that changes in grief but one's attitude toward life. The agony and utter loneliness following the loss of a loved one tear away any illusion that life is impervious to change. This quality of being thrown back on oneself helps clarify values. Priorities shift. The capacity for understanding and appreciating relationships grows. The bereaved often recognizes, with increased awareness, the preciousness of each moment. It is out of these deeper realizations and an enhanced self-awareness that a new sense of meaning arises.

Part VII

When More Help Is Needed

Blessed are they that mourn: for they shall be comforted.

—MATTHEW 5:4

Chapter 17

Grief Therapy and Support Groups

Those who travel the lonely path of grief benefit immensely from the solace provided by others who care. Heartfelt actions of family and friends help to create an environment of understanding and acceptance in which healing grief can take its natural course. However, no matter how nurturing and supportive one's friends, colleagues, and family members may be, there are many in grief who either wish or require additional support and guidance.

Seeking help is not a statement of personal inadequacy; on the contrary, it is often a statement of strength and courage. A professional therapist, support group, or workshop can help the bereaved use the experience of grief to grow, gain deeper insights into themselves, and even accelerate healing.

Fortunately, varied resources are available to help those in grief cope more effectively with the pain and challenge of loss. Each model of care has its benefits and drawbacks. The following is a review of bereavement programs generally available and a clarification of differences between professional and lay assistance.

Psychotherapy, counseling, self-help support groups, grief workshops, and lectures offer a broad range of possibilities to assist those in grief. They have the potential to enhance the bereaved's personal support network by:

- Providing information about the bereavement process.
- Offering nonjudgmental support.
- Encouraging and validating feelings and thoughts.

• Reinforcing positive change.
• Acknowledging signposts of healing.
• Sharing coping techniques.

These venues provide an atmosphere of trust in which the bereaved may ask for assistance without the feeling of imposition they sometimes experience when receiving help from family and friends. The four basic types of bereavement support groups are discussed below.

1. *Professional therapists* including psychiatric physicians, nurses, psychologists, social workers, and others with specialized training have a depth of experience and training that is often crucial for those locked into their grief. See page 212 for a discussion of pathological grief. Treatment may involve individual, group, or family therapy. Such professional support may be time-limited in a series of four to six sessions, often called crisis intervention, or may extend for several months.

Although methods, training, and orientation differ, most mental health professionals have a broad understanding of the problems and strategies available for successful coping in times of profound stress. Despite differences, these professionals share common goals in working with the bereaved: nonjudgmental support, empathy, and a commitment to help the grieving person or family resume adequate functioning and a sense of well-being. Further, medications available through psychiatrists are used in specific situations as an important adjunct to psychotherapy. Individuals may seek help on a private basis assuming there are adequate financial resources and/or insurance coverage. Professional care can also sometimes be found through community mental health clinics at nominal cost or free of charge.

Unfortunately, in spite of increasing public awareness regarding mental health, counseling and psychotherapy often carry a stigma denoting grief as illness. When condoling friends and relations maintain a positive attitude toward the benefits of therapy, their support can go a long way toward encouraging one in grief to seek professional assistance.

2. *Mutual support groups* involve participants, all of whom are actively confronting the issue of their own grief. They are inexpensive and avoid the potential of stigmatizing bereaved individuals as "ill." Such groups can often be found by calling hospitals, churches, your physician, or consulting your local newspaper's directory of events. National organizations can advise you about local chapters and a list of these is found beginning on page 241. The groups may be limited to bereaved or open to bereaved, caregivers, loved ones of the terminally ill, or people who have experienced major loss other than the death of a loved one. Their mainstays are a supportive network of assistance, companionship, understanding participants, and the willingness of members to share their experiences.

Talking with others who have had similar experiences of loss and are at varying stages in the healing process can act as a bridge between the past and the future. These linking relationships offer an opportunity to share social expectations and to exchange coping techniques with persons who have gained understanding from direct experience with similar challenges. Mutual support groups can also be a valuable adjunct to individual psychotherapy.

A word of caution: Mutual support groups depend largely on the foundation of experience and coping skills of more senior members. Such organizations vary widely since there is no outside standard or monitoring of quality. Attending one to three meetings is usually enough to see whether the group appears nurturing, supportive, and appropriate to a potential new member's situation.

3. *Hospice support groups* are offered by hospice organizations and are usually staffed by volunteers under the supervision of a professional. These groups are sometimes restricted to the loved ones of patients who have died under the care of a hospice, but may be open to other members of the community as well. As in mutual support groups, the quality of help varies, but unlike mutual support groups, most hospice bereavement groups utilize trained volunteer

counselors or professionals. The care offered ranges from groups to individual counseling to home visits. Check your yellow pages under Hospice or contact the National Hospice Organization for local referrals (see page 244).

4. *Workshops, conferences, and lectures* are typically one-time programs on the subject of loss or bereavement presented by experts in the field and open to the public. They focus on issues of loss, life transitions, grief, and condolence. Often, they can be an extremely valuable tool, helping those in grief to set their situations in perspective. In addition, workshops and lectures do not carry the stigma of associating bereavement with illness or sickness.

These programs are frequently offered by individuals, college or university extensions, and nonprofit organizations.

Which one of these models will be most helpful depends on individual circumstance. Whatever similarities exist in the nature of the grief experience, each person will take a healing path that is uniquely his or her own. If the bereaved feels ambivalent and is considering counseling, therapy, or a support group, by all means encourage a consultation or trial. For more on the sensitive issue of talking with a bereaved friend or loved one about seeking professional help, see page 212.

Numerous anecdotal accounts from participants, reports from the leaders of support groups and workshops, and the clinical judgment of health-care professionals suggest that for most people *some* assistance is beneficial in coping with the stress of bereavement. One personal story follows.

About seven weeks after her son was killed in a climbing accident, Terry started going to a grief support group. She saw the group listed in a "Community Events" calendar in the local paper and called us for input and encouragement. After some initial hesitation, Terry phoned the church where the group was located and got in touch with the group's leader, a bereavement counselor. Later, she recounted the following story:

After speaking with him, I felt ready to at least take the first step. My friends had been terrific, but now that nearly two months had passed, they seemed, in a natural way, to have found their way back to their own lives. I, on the other hand, was just beginning to feel really lost.

In the group I found a kinship and camaraderie with other bereaved parents that just didn't seem possible with longtime friends. Family and friends and colleagues had all tried, but I could feel how hard it was for them as they fumbled for the right things to say and do.

When I'd tried to talk with friends, they often seemed to listen with discomfort and impatience. Before John's death, I'd never realized how uncomfortable most of us are with silences. We just can't seem to abide a pause of more than, say, three to four seconds.

With other bereaved parents I felt open, free to talk, understood, and supported. Most of all, I didn't feel I was imposing. I could talk and talk and talk. You know, the most important part of the group was the space to talk freely. My friends had often seemed perplexed, even a little concerned, when I repeated myself. But I couldn't help it; at first you have this crazy need to go over it again and again. Each time it seemed to get easier and I felt stronger.

Terry's story is not unusual, either in her hesitation to begin or in her positive experience once having started. Reaching out for help is often very tentative during grief. Those who care will actively support the bereaved's courage and strength to seek assistance during this very stressful, confusing, and challenging time.

Chapter 18

If Grief Is Too Much

If you feel that professional therapy might be helpful for a friend, colleague, or loved one, there are three matters to consider.

1. *How can I tell if therapy is really needed?*

Following the death of a loved one, most bereaved are deeply troubled by their loss and react strongly. In Chapter 2, we discussed at length the varied manifestations of grief. Common reactions to loss, although not bizarre or abnormal during grief, may cause the bereaved to have significant concern for their welfare. Normal grief reactions are sometimes so intense that the bereaved feel they are about to lose control or are "going crazy." Strong and consistent reassurance from friends and loved ones is often all that they need. However, there are certain grief reactions that may benefit from or even require professional help.

As a nonprofessional, you may be hesitant to make a judgment in this area. But as a caring friend, co-worker, or family member, your sensitive perceptions and opinions can be invaluable at a time when the bereaved may be unclear and insecure. Although most people meet the challenge of grief and are thereby enriched by those they have loved and lost, a few others are trapped in the web of grief for a prolonged period. They are caught between a past life that can't be reclaimed and a future that has yet to be lived.

Studies have demonstrated that individuals are at higher risk for problems in the grief process when they have a background of mental instability, serious and chronic medical problems, or if they had a troubled or highly dependent relationship with the deceased. Other risk factors that increase the potential for a pathological grief response include the existence of additional life stresses such as divorce or loss of employment, or the lack of a substantial support network of friends and/or family. If the grief follows the death of a child or any violent death, there is also increased risk of greater upheaval in bereavement.

It is far too simple to label individuals who have these risk factors as candidates for "abnormal" grief responses. Many in these circumstances have perfectly healthy grief responses. At the same time, those without risk factors are not immune to troubled courses of grief.

If your friend or relative moves from one phase of grief to another, even though there will be steps backward and forward along the way, you can assume the bereaved is progressing in a healthy manner through the grief process. What, then, would alert you to a potential situation of so-called pathological grief?

There are several specific manifestations that should trigger your special concern. In the presence of any of these, a professional consultation should be encouraged to determine whether or not therapy or counseling is indicated. Pathological grief is not a separate set of grief responses; rather it is an intensification, a prolongation, or an inhibition of normal grief. Again, see Chapter 2 for a review of the phases of grief.

Consider a referral for professional consultation if the bereaved exhibits sustained changes in behavior that are intensely experienced. *Sustained* is the key signal since many of these changes are expected and normal during grief, but only temporary in duration. The length that symptoms exist varies greatly, but for our purposes, any of the following symptoms that are sustained with lasting intensity for six to eight weeks deserve careful scrutiny:

- Major deterioration in hygiene habits
- Difficulty in simple decision making
- Expressions of fear, anger, or guilt
- Hyperactivity or compulsive talking

- Memory problems and confusion
- Concern over hallucinations (seeing or hearing things that are not actually present)
- Major disturbance of self-esteem, preoccupation with worthlessness, and self-condemnation
- Depression or withdrawal
- Significant impairment in social functioning
- Initiating or increasing drug and/or alcohol abuse
- Physical complaints or symptoms including failure to eat, continued weight loss, extreme problems sleeping

Although you may recognize that psychotherapy can benefit anyone in grief, the decision to begin therapy can only be made by the bereaved themselves. *If, however, there are threats of suicide, homicide, or self-mutilation, and the person refuses to seek help, your decision to act should be different.* These three issues cry out for professional help. Your responsibility should be to take definitive steps and immediately inform an appropriate party. This may be a parent, spouse, physician, member of the clergy, or the police. You may be afraid that your intervention will be construed as betraying confidentiality, but such actions grow out of your respect, concern, and compassion and have an integrity all their own.

2. *How do I approach my friend with my concerns?*

Approaching the subject of lay or professional assistance for one in grief can be quite delicate. If you have reason to feel that some form of additional help is needed, openness, honesty, clarity, and support are the gifts you can offer. Here is one possible approach:

> As I continue to see how badly you feel I'm concerned enough to tell you my thoughts. I hope you can hear them. It feels as if I'm unable to give you the support, help, and guidance you need in this terribly difficult time. You have my caring and my love, but as your friend I also want to tell you that it seems that some other input or help might be very worthwhile.

> I don't plan to stop my support, but I want to be honest and suggest that you consider a professional consultation just to get an objective opinion about the situation/exploring a self-help grief recovery group/or talking with your minister. I have a couple of names we might look over together if you're interested.

This sensitive area, suggesting professional help, is one where semantics can be very important. If you feel the bereaved should see a professional rather than go to a self-help group, it is far more appropriate for you to suggest a referral for a professional consultation—not therapy. A consultation is simply a request for professional input. Of course, if the bereaved brings up the subject of some sort of outside assistance, your role becomes much easier.

You may wish to do some research on local resources before mentioning the subject to your friend. If so, do not give out the name of the bereaved when making inquiries. If you have made such inquiries, be honest with the bereaved about them.

Of course, it is possible that the bereaved will react to your suggestion with anger or denial of the need for help. If this happens, don't take the bereaved's response personally. Remember that this is someone who is not only deeply involved in grief, but who is having difficulty coping with the process. Although the bereaved may have recognized this difficulty, your intervention may trigger embarrassment, and our response to embarrassment is often anger. Second, don't plead your case; therapy is of questionable value to anyone not committed to the process. Third, realize that while your suggestion may not be heard or appreciated in the moment, you have planted a seed that may later bear fruit. The risks of speaking out are real, but the benefits may be vast, and a caring friend is willing to take a chance.

3. *How do I find a good therapist or counselor?*

Once a decision has been made to seek outside help in resolving the bereaved's grief, finding a good therapist or counselor is crucial. You can be very supportive if you are willing to do the footwork for your bereaved friend. This may take a little doing, but remember that those in grief, especially those who are having difficulty in resolving their grief, may find even simple tasks difficult. This, combined with a feeling of embarrassment at needing help, can make the prospect of researching potential therapists paralyzing. Those helped by grief therapy have often shared with us their gratitude toward friends and relations who eased the way and helped them take their first steps toward full recovery from the trauma of loss.

How to begin? The best source is often a therapist you know and trust. If you aren't acquainted with local professionals, word of mouth may provide excellent referrals, especially when such referrals come from talking with others who have been in grief therapy with positive results. Again, unless the bereaved has given permission for you to do so, do not mention his or her name when making general inquiries. If no one with whom you have personal contact is able to assist, there are many other options:

- Local professional organizations of psychiatrists, psychologists, and social workers are listed in the yellow pages. They often have screened referral lists, sometimes citing those who specialize in different areas such as grief therapy.
- Colleges and universities may have departments of psychiatry, psychology, or social work. Ask to talk to the chairperson.
- Call the grief and hospice support groups in your community to find names of competent therapists.
- Other potential referral sources include county mental health organizations, your own physician, minister, or rabbi, and local school guidance counselors or school psychologists.

Grief therapy or counseling is an area of special interest, skill, and experience. It is perfectly acceptable to make appointments for a first interview with two or three therapists. This will allow the bereaved to choose the one with whom he or she feels most comfortable. We also suggest that the bereaved ask several key questions:

1. What is your training, background, or experience in working with patients or clients in grief?
2. Are you able to and under what circumstances might you arrange for prescription medications?
3. Is your practice restricted to one-to-one therapy or do you also work with groups?
4. What is your feeling about additional participation in mutual support groups?
5. What is your usual fee and do you have a sliding scale?
6. Do you take insurance? Which companies?

As therapy begins, it may be helpful in supporting your bereaved friends to remind them that while some aspects of therapy may be painful, they should feel helped by the process. If after two to four sessions they do not feel supported, understood, or treated with dignity, compassion, and respect, they should not give up the notion of therapy but seek someone else for another trial. This in no way implies failure on the part of the bereaved, but in their fragile state they may feel that it does. Again, it's a time when your support for the courage to seek help can have a profound impact on the forward progress of the healing process.

Final Thoughts for Those Who Help: The Limits of Compassion

> Love, like the ocean,
> is vast and forever,
> And sorrow, but a shadow
> that moves over the sea.
>
> —John Gray

It seems simple, but truth often is. Although we like to think our compassion has no bounds, it does. We may burn with a desire to help and to heal, but that same burning can be all-consuming. If we give and give without replenishing ourselves and overextend the limits of compassion, we may be left with nothing left to give. What was nurturing becomes a burden; what was heartfully given becomes a forced effort.

To serve another during a time of loss with commitment and dedication can be a personal blessing, but it also requires time and energy. Certainly, by giving with an open heart, we receive; our soul is nurtured. Yet there is a danger. "Compassion fatigue," "condolers' overload," and "burnout" are names for a condition that sometimes affects lay as well as professional caregivers. It strikes those who take on too heavy a load of other's burdens, leaving little time or energy for themselves. If they are not alert to their limitations, condolers may become disillusioned, irritable, and depressed. They may work too much, sleep too little, and sacrifice their own life and families for others.

Four simple guidelines help us, as condolers, to maintain balance and productively rekindle our energies.

1. *Be honest with yourself and the bereaved.* This is one of the most important challenges to be met in condoling. By taking care of yourself and openly communicating your needs to the bereaved, you may inspire them to do the same. Most in grief will also welcome your acknowledging your own limits. When you do this, you support them in doing likewise. They are less likely to be uncomfortable asking for help if they know that you are clear when enough is enough. Your generosity may be destined for failure if it becomes forced and thus insincere. If you feel depleted and burdened you may trigger feelings of guilt and anxiety in the bereaved as they experience your distress.

2. *Draw on supports that nurture you.* During a period of dedicated condoling it is important to renew your energy, keep up your health, and maintain a positive attitude. Draw on supports that nurture you including friends, work, religion, meditation, reading, exercise, and recreation. Don't wait until you feel burned out and exhausted emotionally and physically. Rather, set aside time for yourself to do what you enjoy and what energizes you. Just as it is important for the bereaved, it is important for you to have a healthy diet and get sufficient rest.

3. *Be alert to emotional mirroring.* There is always some interplay of emotions in any intense human interaction. Not uncommonly, sensitive condolers may take on and experience the moods and feelings of the bereaved. Anger, loneliness, irritability, sadness, emptiness, helplessness, and frustration may be directly felt by the condoler. Also, involvement with a bereaved person often rekindles memories and feelings of our own prior losses and can trigger anniversary-like reactions in ourselves. By taking care of yourself and

being alert to this potential mirror effect, you are likely to maintain a sense of balance and perspective in your own life.

4. *Don't place yourself in the role of rescuer.* Avoid acting like a rescuer and treating the bereaved like a victim. This can be demeaning to the bereaved, reflects a certain arrogance on your part, and usually reaps resentment and not gratitude. Also, avoid becoming so identified with the bereaved that you try to grieve *for* them. The healing work of grief is a walk along a narrow path that only has room for one. A surrogate, no matter how well intended, cannot and will not accomplish anything. It is the bereaved's challenge and responsibility. Give each person in mourning the respect and the dignity to recognize that, as much as you want to help, grief is not your work but theirs.

Responding heartfully to one in grief possesses vast potential to deepen our understanding, sympathy, and courage, and to enlarge our visions. The cautions are there but so are the rewards. Condoling helps us to build a stronger foundation of coping abilities in order to face more openly the losses that are around the corner in our own life. When you truly listen to friends in grief, when you serve them not out of social form but out of a natural outpouring of feeling, you are likely to experience a kinship with humanity. Then, too, when we condole with another over the loss of a loved one we are reminded of the preciousness of life and often find ourselves reassessing our own priorities. Ultimately, service to those in grief teaches us about the power, the mystery, and the value of relationships.

Quotations Through Time: Words of Tender Understanding

> Like a bird
> Singing in the rain,
> Let grateful memories
> Survive in time of sorrow.
>
> —Robert Louis Stevenson

Few of us find it easy to combine, especially in just a sentence or two, words that are able to express to others the feelings in our heart. The authors of the following quotations have striven to do just that: to give form to the face of sorrow, to share a certain sensitivity, to encourage the recognition of personal truths. They have done this with elegance and grace in words that resonate within us. We may not agree with each sentiment expressed; we may even recoil when others' visions of life and death run counter to our own. But this gallery of poetic miniatures invites us to stroll through the halls of shared human experience, to look—both outside and in—and to be touched by the brush of another's heart.

For easy reference, the quotations have been divided into four categories: From the Bible, From the East, From Shakespeare, and General Quotations. In themselves, many of these quotations are inspirational, and as several of the sample letters in earlier chapters illustrate, such quotations may be the seed for letters of condolence that have the power to help and to heal, to light moments of darkness.

FROM THE BIBLE

The Lord is my shepherd; I shall not want.
He maketh me to lie down in green pastures:
He leadeth me beside the still waters.
He restoreth my soul:
He leadeth me in the paths of righteousness
for his name's sake.
Yea, though I walk through the valley of the
shadow of death, I will fear no evil:
For thou art with me; thy rod and thy staff
they comfort me.
Thou preparest a table before me in the presence
of mine enemies:
Thou anointest my head with oil; my cup runneth over.
Surely goodness and mercy shall follow me all
the days of my life:
And I will dwell in the house of the Lord
for ever.

—PSALMS 23

He healeth the broken in heart.

—PSALMS 147:3

He hath said, I will never leave thee, nor forsake thee.

—HEBREWS 13:5

Cast your burden on the Lord, and He will sustain you.

—PSALMS 55:22

Make bitter weeping, and make passionate wailing, and let thy mourning be according to his desert, and so be comforted for thy sorrow. For of sorrow cometh death, and sorrow of heart will bow down the strength. . . . Give not thy heart unto unending sorrow: put it away, remembering the last end: forget it not, for there is no returning again: him thou shalt not profit, and thou wilt hurt thyself. Remember, for him it was yesterday, and today for thee.

—ECCLESIASTICUS 38:17

Thou shalt come to thy grave in a full age, like as a shock of corn cometh in his season.

—JOB 5:26

Blessed are they that mourn: for they shall be comforted.

—MATTHEW 5:4

As one whom his mother comforteth, so will I comfort you; and ye shall be comforted.

—ISAIAH 66:13

Wait on the Lord: be of good courage, and he will strengthen thine heart: wait, I say, on the Lord.

—PSALMS 27:14

I have heard thy prayer, I have seen thy tears.

—ISAIAH 38:5

Fear thou not, for I am with thee; be not dismayed, for I am thy God: I will strengthen thee; yea, I will help thee; yea, I will uphold thee with the right hand of my righteousness.

—ISAIAH 41:10

Blessed be God . . . the Father of mercies, and the God of all comfort; who comforteth us in all our tribulation, that we may be able to comfort them which are in any trouble, by the comfort wherewith we ourselves are comforted of God.

—2 CORINTHIANS 1:3,4

I am the resurrection, and the life: he that believeth in me, though he were dead, yet shall he live: and whosoever . . . believeth on me shall never die.

—JOHN 11:25,26

And ye therefore now have sorrow: but I shall see you again, and your heart shall rejoice, and your joy no one taketh away from you.

—JOHN 16:22

And God shall wipe away all tears from their eyes; and there shall be no more death, neither sorrow, nor crying, neither shall there be any more pain: for the former things are passed away.

—REVELATION 21:4

And we know that all things work together for good to them that love God.

—ROMANS 8:28

FROM THE EAST

Let me not pray to be sheltered from
dangers but to be fearless in facing
them.
Let me not beg for the stilling of
my pain but for the heart to conquer
it.

—RABINDRANATH TAGORE

I walk as one walks in cold winter in a cold stream. Everybody is certain except me. I am uncertain, I hesitate. I cannot claim knowledge because all is so mysterious.

—LAO TZU

For life and death are one,
even as the river and the sea are one.

—KAHLIL GIBRAN

There are no answers in this lifetime. And that is it.

—DA FREE JOHN

We don't know life: how can we know death?

—CONFUCIUS

The world rushes on over the strings of the lingering heart making the music of sadness.

—Rabindranath Tagore

The world of dew is
A world of dew, yet even
So, yet even so . . .

—Issa
(composed shortly after the death of the author's only child)

A solemn funeral is inconceivable to the Chinese mind.

—Lin Yutang

And ever has it been that love knows not
its own depth until the hour of separation.

—Kahlil Gibran

The storm of the last night has crowned this morning with golden peace.

—Rabindranath Tagore

Concealed grief has no remedy.

—Turkish Proverb

And you would accept the seasons of your heart,
even as you have always accepted the seasons
that pass over your fields.
And you would watch with serenity
through the winters of your grief.

—Kahlil Gibran

One of the best means for arousing the wish to work on yourself is to realize that you may die at any moment. But first you must learn how to keep it in mind.

—George Gurdjieff

The past and the unknown do not meet at any point; they cannot be brought together by any act whatsoever; there is no bridge to cross over nor a path that leads to it. The two have never met and will never meet. The past has to cease for the unknowable, for that immensity to be.

—J. KRISHNAMURTI

Your pain is the breaking of the shell
that encloses your understanding.

—KAHLIL GIBRAN

We do not know what anything is. The summarization of our existence is Mystery, absolute, unqualified confrontation with what we cannot know. And no matter how sophisticated we become by experience, this will always be true of us.

—DA FREE JOHN

If I am to eliminate my own sufferings, I must act in the knowledge that I exist in dependent relationships with other human beings and the whole of nature.

—H. H. DALAI LAMA

And could you keep your heart in wonder at the daily miracles in your life, your pain would not seem less wondrous than your joy.

—KAHLIL GIBRAN

I shan't die, I shan't go anywhere,
I'll be here;
But don't ask me anything,
I shan't answer.

—DEATH VERSE OF MASTER IKKYU

Religion is not asking. It is a longing of the soul.

—GANDHI

Disciple: Is there no afterlife? What about punishment for our sins?
Lama Thubten Yeshe: Why not enjoy your chocolate?
Your life is here and now. Birth is not a beginning; death is not an end.

—Lama Thubten Yeshe

Death . . . is the name given to a change which comes when one leaves the coarse atmosphere of the earth and enters a finer one of Light. Something like the sun setting in one place and rising in another.

—Kirpal Singh

Why do you mourn the loss of your parents? I shall tell you where they are: they are only within ourselves and are ourselves. For the life-current has passed through innumerable incarnations, births and deaths, pleasures and pains . . . just as the water current in a river flows over rocks, pits, sands, elevations, and depressions on its way, but still the current is unaffected.

—Sri Ramana Maharshi

Disciples, there is a realm in which there is neither earth nor water, fire nor air; not endless space, infinite consciousness, not nothingness; not perceptions nor nonperceptions. In it there is neither this world nor another, neither sun nor moon. I call it neither a coming nor a going nor a standing still; not death, nor birth; it is without basis, change, or stability. Disciples, it is the end of sorrow.

—Gautama Buddha

The morning glory blooms but for an hour
and yet it differs not at heart
from the giant pine
that lives for a thousand years.

—Teitoku Matsunaga

Whatever comes will go. Whatever goes will come.

—YOGIRAJ SRI SWAMI SATCHIDANANDA

FROM SHAKESPEARE

Grief would have tears,
and sorrow bids me speak.

—ALL'S WELL THAT ENDS WELL, Act III, sc. 4

Give sorrow words; the grief that
does not speak
Whispers the o'er-fraught heart
and bids it break.

—MACBETH, Act IV, sc. 3

Now cracks a noble heart.
Goodnight, sweet prince,
And flights of angels sing thee to thy rest!

—HAMLET, Act V, sc. 2

You do surely bar the door upon your own liberty, if you deny your griefs to your friend.

—HAMLET, Act III, sc. 2

My heart is drown'd with grief,
Whose flood begins to flow within mine eyes.

—II HENRY VI, Act III, sc. 1

Grief has so wrought on him,
He takes false shadows for true substances.

—TITUS ANDRONICUS, Act III, sc. 2

Every one can master grief but he that has it.

—MUCH ADO ABOUT NOTHING, Act III, sc. 2

Each substance of a grief hath twenty shadows,
Which shows like grief itself, but is not so.

—Richard II, Act II, sc. 2

My tongue cannot express my grief.

—Venus and Adonis l. 1069

Tis very true, my grief lies all within;
And these external manners of laments
Are merely shadows to the unseen grief
That swells with silence in the tortured soul.

—Richard II, Act IV, sc. 1

King Philip: You are as fond of grief as of your child.
Constance: Grief fills the room up of my absent child,
Lies in his bed, walks up and down with me.
Puts on his pretty looks, repeats his words,
Remembers me of all his gracious parts,
Stuffs out his vacant garments with his form;
Then, have I reason to be fond of grief?

—King John, Act III, sc. 4

GENERAL QUOTATIONS

Though nothing can bring back the hour
Of Splendour in the grass, of glory in the flower;
We will grieve not, rather find
Strength in what remains behind;
In the primal sympathy
Which having been must ever be;
In the soothing thoughts that spring
Out of human suffering;
In the faith that looks through death,
In the years that bring the philosophic mind.

—William Wordsworth

Life is real! Life is earnest!
And the grave is not its goal;
Dust thou art, to dust returnest,
Was not spoken of the soul.

—H. W. LONGFELLOW

Love, like the ocean,
is vast and forever,
And sorrow, but a shadow
that moves over the sea.

—JOHN GRAY

Life must go on;
I forget just why.

—EDNA ST. VINCENT MILLAY

Still there are moments when one feels free from one's own identification with human limitations and inadequacies. At such moments, one imagines that one stands on some spot of a small planet, gazing in amazement at the cold yet profoundly moving beauty of the eternal, the unfathomable: life and death flow into one, and there is neither evolution nor destiny; only being.

—ALBERT EINSTEIN

Life's race well run,
Life's work well done,
Life's victory won,
Now cometh rest.

—JOHN MILLS

The highest tribute to the dead is not grief, but gratitude.

—THORNTON WILDER

If you can meet with triumph and disaster
And treat those two imposters just the same . . .
Yours is the Earth and everything that's in it . . .

—RUDYARD KIPLING

The distance that the dead
have gone
Does not at first appear
Their coming back seems
possible
For many an ardent year.

—EMILY DICKINSON

Grief is a tree that has tears for its fruit.

—PHILEMON

In life he walked with God and in death, God will surely walk with him.

—ANONYMOUS

It is the great mystery of human life that old grief gradually passes into quiet, tender joy. The mild serenity of age takes the place of the riotous blood of youth. I bless the rising sun each day, and, as before, my heart sings to meet it, but now I love even more its setting, its long slanting rays and the soft, tender, gentle memories that come with them, the dear images from the whole of my long, happy life—and over all the Divine Truth, softening, reconciling, forgiving!

—FYODOR DOSTOEVSKY

All griefs with bread are less.

—GEORGE HERBERT

There is a destiny that makes us brothers;
None goes his way alone:
All that we send into the lives of others
Comes back into our own.

—EDWIN MARKHAM

Grief has a natural eloquence . . . and breaks out in more moving sentiments than can be supplied by the finest imagination.

—JOSEPH ADDISON

Come not, when I am dead,
To drop the foolish tears upon my grave,
To trample round my fallen head,
And vex the unhappy dust thou wouldst not save.
There let the wind sweep and the plover cry;
But thou, go by.

—ALFRED TENNYSON

Wail not for precious chance passed away,
Weep not for golden ages on the wane!
Each night I burn the records of the day;
At sunrise every soul is born again . . .
Art thou a mourner? Rouse thee from thy spell . . .
Each morning gives thee wings to flee from hell,
Each night a star to guide thy feet to Heaven.

—WALTER MALONE

There is no grief like the grief which does not speak.

—H. W. LONGFELLOW

The dark today leads into light tomorrow;
There is no endless joy,
. . . and yet no endless sorrow.

—ELLA WHEELER WILCOX

In my happier days I used to remark on the aptitude of the saying, "When in life we are in the midst of death." I have since learnt that it's more apt to say, "When in death we are in the midst of life."

—A SURVIVOR OF THE BELSEN CONCENTRATION CAMP

Those who have known grief seldom seem sad.

—BENJAMIN DISRAELI

This world is not conclusion;
A sequel stands beyond,
Invisible, as music,
But positive,
As sound.

—EMILY DICKINSON

Condolence is the art of giving courage.

—MONICA LEHNER-KAHN

My answer to Saint Paul's question "O death, where is thy sting?" is Saint Paul's own answer: "The sting of death is sin." The sin that I mean is the sin of selfishly failing to wish to survive the death of someone with whose life my own life is bound up. This is selfish because the sting of death is less sharp for the person who dies than it is for the bereaved survivor. This is, as I see it, the capital fact about the relation between living and dying.

—ARNOLD TOYNBEE

Earth has no sorrow that heaven cannot heal.

—THOMAS MOORE

God seemed to have made him just what he was that he might be a blessing to others, and when the influence of his character and abilities began to be felt, removed him. These are Mysteries, my Dear, that we cannot contemplate without astonishment, but which will nevertheless be explained hereafter, and must in the mean time be revered in silence.

—WILLIAM COWPER

This is my last message to you: in sorrow seek happiness.

—FYODOR DOSTOEVSKY

After the night is done;
Life brings the sweet with the bitter,
Laughter will follow tears,
Just as after the snows of winter,
The glory of springtime appears!

—THOMAS MALLOY

I walked a mile with Sorrow and ne'er a word said she;
But, oh, the things I learned from her
When Sorrow walked with me.

—ROBERT BROWNING

Real love doesn't die. It's the physical body that dies. Genuine, authentic love has no expectations whatsoever; it doesn't even need the physical presence of a person. . . . Even when he is dead and buried that part of you that loves the person will always live.

—ELISABETH KÜBLER-ROSS

To fear death, gentlemen, is nothing other than to think oneself wise when one is not; for it is to think one knows what one does not know. No man knows whether death may not even turn out to be the greatest of blessings for a human being; and yet people fear it as if they knew for certain that it is the greatest of evils.

—SOCRATES

To live in hearts we leave behind is not to die.

—W. W. CAMPBELL

A little soul scarce fledged for earth
Takes wing with heaven again for goal
Even while we hailed as fresh from birth
A little soul.

—ALGERNON SWINBURNE

Can I see another's woe
And not be in sorrow too?
Can I see another's grief,
And not seek for kind relief?

—William Blake

The change from being to becoming seems to be birth, and the change from becoming to being seems to be death; but in reality no one is ever born, nor does one ever die.

—Apollonius of Tyana

When you look back at the anguish, suffering, and traumas in your life, you'll see that these are the periods of biggest growth. After a loss that brings you dreadfully painful months, you are a different man, a different woman. Many years later, they will be able to look back and see the positive things—togetherness in their family, faith or whatever—that came out of their pain.

—Elisabeth Kübler-Ross

Children's griefs are little, certainly; but so is the child, so is its endurance, so is its field of vision, while its nervous impressionability is keener than ours. Grief is a matter of relativity; the sorrow should be estimated by its proportion to the sorrower; a gash is as painful to one as an amputation to another.

—Francis Thompson

Were it possible for us to see further than our knowledge reaches, and yet a little way beyond the outworks of our divination, perhaps we would then endure our sorrows with greater confidence than our joys. For they are the moments when something new has entered us, something unknown; our feelings grow mute in shy perplexity, everything in us withdraws, a stillness comes, and the new, which no one knows, stands in the midst of it and is silent.

—Rainer Maria Rilke

You must not shut the night inside you,
But endlessly in light the dark immerse.
A tiny lamp has gone out in my tent—
I bless the flame that warms the universe.

—FRIEDRICH RÜCKERT

These are the gifts I ask
Of Thee, Spirit serene:
Strength for the daily task,
Courage to face the road,
Good cheer to help me bear the traveler's load,
And, for the hours of rest that come between,
An inward joy of all things heard and seen.

—HENRY VAN DYKE

Let me do my work each day;
And if the darkened hours of despair overcome me,
May I not forget the strength that comforted me
In the desolation of other times.
May I still remember the bright hours that found me
Walking over the silent hills of my childhood,
Or dreaming on the margin of the quiet river,
When a light glowed within me,
And I promised my early God to have courage
Amid the tempests of the changing years.

—MAX EHRMANN

The ocean has her ebbings—so has grief.

—THOMAS CAMPBELL

Abide with me: fast falls the eventide;
The darkness deepens; Lord, with me abide:
When other helpers fail, and comforts flee,
Help of the helpless, O abide with me.

—HENRY F. LYTE

Every blade in the field—
  Every leaf in the forest—
Lays down its life
  in its season
as beautifully
  as it was taken up.

—Henry David Thoreau

In this sad world of ours, sorrow comes to all . . .
It comes with bitterest agony . . .
Perfect relief is not possible, except with time.
You cannot now realize that you will ever feel better . . .
And yet this is a mistake.
You are sure to be happy again,
To know this, which is certainly true,
Will make you come less miserable now.
I have experienced enough to know what I say.

—Abraham Lincoln

(Three of Lincoln's sons died during his lifetime.)

Death destroys the body, as the scaffolding is destroyed after the building is up and finished. And he whose building is up rejoices at the destruction of the scaffolding and of the body.

—Leo Tolstoy

Life is a mystery to be lived,
  not a problem to be solved.

—Osho

Recommended Resources

Mutual support and self-help groups exist in many cities. The following is a list of national organizations, most of which have chapters throughout the United States. They may be contacted for local referrals. The list is always changing. To locate other resources in your community, consider calling churches and synagogues, hospital departments of psychiatry, psychology, and social service, state and local mental health departments, school personnel, community centers, and funeral directors.

Organizations and Mutual Support Groups

For Widowed Persons

THEOS (They Help Each Other Spiritually)
Office Building Suite 306
Penns Hill Mall
Pittsburgh, PA 15235

WIDOWED PERSONS SERVICE
American Association of Retired Persons
1909 K Street N.W.
Washington, DC 20049
The *Widowed Person Service Directory* lists nearly 400 groups nationwide.

NATIONAL ASSOCIATION FOR WIDOWED PEOPLE
P.O. Box 3564
Springfield, IL 62708

For Parents

THE COMPASSIONATE FRIENDS
P.O. Box 3696
Oak Brook, IL 60522-3696

CANDLELIGHTERS CHILDHOOD CANCER FOUNDATION
2025 Eye Street N.W., Suite 1011
Washington, DC 20006

PARENTS OF MURDERED CHILDREN
100 E. 8th Street, B-41
Cincinnati, OH 45202

ROTHMAN-COLE CENTER FOR SIBLING LOSS
The Southern School
1456 West Montrose
Chicago, IL 60613

NATIONAL FOUNDATION FOR SUDDEN INFANT DEATH (SIDS)
1501 Broadway
New York, NY 10036

NATIONAL SUDDEN INFANT DEATH SYNDROME FOUNDATION
8240 Professional Place
2 Metro Plaza, Suite 205
Landover, MD 20785

FOR CHILDREN

School Counseling Departments

When a child is in grief, we strongly recommend that the child's school counseling department be contacted. Many school districts have professionals on staff who can provide grief counseling or who are aware of local experts and/or support groups. In addition, informing the child's teachers of the loss broadens the grieving child's support system.

Centers for Grieving Children

In some states, programs exist to provide specialized assistance for children in grief. Programs such as The Dougy Center in Portland, Oregon, Camp Amanda in Des Moines, Iowa, The Warm Place in Fort Worth, Texas, and Fernside in Cincinnati, Ohio, offer these important services. Again, your child's school counselor is a good first source of information.

For Families and Friends of Victims of Violent Death

FAMILIES OF HOMICIDE VICTIMS
2 Lafayette Street
New York, NY 10007

MOTHERS AGAINST DRUNK DRIVING (MADD)
669 Airport Freeway, Suite 310
Hurst, TX 76053
Victim Line 1-800-438-MADD

For Families and Friends of Suicide Victims

SURVIVORS OF SUICIDE (SOS)
c/o Fr. Arnaldo Pagrazzi, Chaplain
St. Joseph's Hospital
5000 W. Chambers Street
Milwaukee, WI 53210

SEASONS: SUICIDE BEREAVEMENT, INC.
4777 Maniloa Drive
Salt Lake City, UT 84117

AMERICAN ASSOCIATION OF SUICIDOLOGY
2459 S. Ash
Denver, CO 80222
For a comprehensive state-by-state list of support groups

for those living through the aftermath of suicide, refer to *Silent Grief* by Christopher Lukas and Henry M. Seiden, Ph.D. (Bantam, 1990).

For Families and Friends of AIDS Victims

NATIONAL ASSOCIATION OF PEOPLE WITH AIDS
1012 14th Street, Suite 601
Washington, DC 20005

General Interest

NATIONAL ASSOCIATION FOR MENTAL HEALTH
1800 N. Kent Street
Arlington, VA 22209

NATIONAL HOSPICE ORGANIZATION
1901 N. Fort Meyer Drive, Suite 402
Arlington, VA 22209

THE NEPTUNE SOCIETY
1275 Columbus Avenue
San Francisco, CA 94133
(for funeral alternatives)

Professional Organizations (for referral to grief therapists)

AMERICAN PSYCHIATRIC ASSOCIATION
1700 18th Street
Washington, DC 20009

AMERICAN PSYCHOLOGICAL ASSOCIATION
1200 17th Street N.W.
Washington, DC 20036

NATIONAL ASSOCIATION OF SOCIAL WORKERS
1425 H Street N.W.
Washington, DC 20005

American Association of Marriage
and Family Therapists
1100 17th Street N.W., 12th Floor
Washington, DC 20036

Suggested Readings

For the Bereaved

Gift Books

Gibran, Kahlil. *The Prophet.* New York: Knopf, 1960.
Classic and inspiring work touching many aspects of life and death.

Grollman, Earl A. *Living When a Loved One has Died.* Boston: Beacon Press, 1977.
Brief, reassuring, and positive free verse gently helps the reader to understand and work through grief.

Rodegast, Pat, and Judith Stanton. *Emmanuel's Book.* New York: Bantam, 1987.
Wise and sensitive words about the search for meaning, growth, and change.

Saint-Exupery, Antoine de. *The Little Prince.* New York: Harcourt, Brace & World, 1943.
Timeless, charming, and provocative tale of life's challenges, told through the adventures of a wide-eyed young boy. For all ages.

Whitaker, Agnes (ed.). *All in the End Is Harvest.* London: Darton, Longman and Todd, 1984.
An anthology of readings and poetry for those who grieve.

Williams, Marjorie. *The Velveteen Rabbit.* New York: Doubleday and Company, 1969.
Beautifully illustrated and tender story about love and death, written from the point of view of a toy rabbit. For all ages.

Personal and Inspiring Reflections

Caine, Lynn. *Widow.* New York: Macmillan, 1974.
Best-selling personal memoir.

Grollman, Earl A. (ed.). *What Helped Me When My Loved One Died.* Boston: Beacon Press, 1981.
Intimate stories from those who have suffered the loss of a loved one. Includes a wide range of relationships.

Gunther, John. *Death Be Not Proud.* New York: Harper & Row, 1949.
A father's account of the death of his son.

Lewis, C. S. *A Grief Observed.* New York: The Seabury Press, 1963.
Provocative and insightful journal chronicling the author's grief experience following the death of his wife.

Lindbergh, Ann Morrow. *Hour of Gold, Hour of Lead.* New York: Harcourt Brace Jovanovich, 1973.
Deeply moving, radiant, and somber, Lindbergh's book reflects on diaries and letters pertaining to her life before, during, and after the renowned kidnapping and murder of her child. Includes a memorable essay on the nature of grief.

Nouwen, Henri J. M. *A Letter of Consolation.* New York: Harper & Row, 1982.
Inspiring letter of condolence written by a priest to his father after the death of the priest's mother.

Coping and the Grief Process

Caine, Lynn. *Lifelines.* New York: Doubleday, 1977.
A blend of personal testimony, holistic philosophy, and practical advice written by the author of *Widow.*

Caine, Lynn. *Being a Widow.* New York: William Morrow and Company, Inc., 1988.
Well-written self-help guide full of sound advice and practical strategies.

Krauss, Pesach, and Morrie Goldfischer. *Why Me? Coping with Grief, Loss, and Change.* New York: Bantam Books, 1988.
Insights into grief and the effects of illness and hospitalization as told by a rabbi.

Kushner, Harold J. *When Bad Things Happen to Good People.* New York: Schocken Books, 1981.
A rabbi deals clearly and sensitively with the problems of human suffering.

Lord, Janice Harris. *No Time for Goodbyes: Coping with Sorrow, Anger and Injustice After a Tragic Death.* Ventura: Pathfinder Publishing, 1987.
Techniques for coping with homicide and violent death. Also addresses related topics including attorneys, trials, and financial difficulties.

Lukas, Christopher, and Henry M. Seiden, Ph. D. *Silent Grief: Living in the Wake of Suicide.* New York: Bantam, 1990.
A moving, comprehensive, and practical guide to help those left behind.

Manning, Doug. *Don't Take My Grief Away.* New York: Harper & Row, 1984.
Practical and consoling guide for those who have lost a loved one. Begins with extensive discussion of funeral decisions.

Myers, Edward. *When Parents Die—A Guide for Adults.* New York: Viking Penguin, 1986.
Practical suggestions and commentary on the loss of a parent.

Nieberg, Herbert, and Arlene Fischer. *Pet Loss: A Thoughtful Guide for Adults and Children.* New York: Harper & Row, 1982.
Excellent and comprehensive review of the impact of the death of a pet. Appropriate for pet owners and professionals alike.

Nudel, Adele Rice. *Starting Over: Help for Young Widows and Widowers.* New York: Dodd, Mead, 1986.
Practical suggestions and workable options for bereaved spouses.

O'Connor, Nancy. *Letting Go with Love: The Grieving Process.* Apache Junction, AZ: La Mariposa Press, 1984.
Readable, practical, and supportive approach to facing loss and change.

Schiff, Harriet Sarnoff. *The Bereaved Parent.* New York: Crown Publishers, 1977.
Thoughtful, practical, and reassuring guide to help parents cope with each facet of their grief.

Schmidt, Judith Sara. *How to Cope with Grief.* New York: Ballantine, 1989.
A "thought-a-week" guide offering advice and suggestions for moving through grief.

Staudacher, Carol. *Beyond Grief.* Oakland, CA: New Harbinger Publications, Inc., 1987.
A how-to book to assist the bereaved to cope and find resolution to their grief.

Stearns, Ann Kaiser. *Living Through Personal Crisis.* New York: Ballantine, 1985.
Excellent work with extensive practical suggestions.

Tatelbaum, Judy. *The Courage to Grieve.* New York: Harper & Row, 1980.
Outstanding and practical guide for those in grief.

Tatelbaum, Judy. *You Don't Have to Suffer.* New York: Harper & Row, 1989.
Handbook for moving beyond life's crises to find ways of diminishing personal suffering through forgiveness and commitment.

Veninga, Robert. *A Gift of Hope: How We Survive Our Tragedies.* New York: Ballantine Books, 1986.
Approaches to facing major life crises, including grief.

Viorst, Judith. *Necessary Losses.* New York: Simon and Schuster, 1986.
"The loves, illusions, dependencies and impossible expectations that all of us have to give up in order to grow."

Westberg, Granger. *Good Grief*. Philadelphia: Fortress Press, 1962.
Best-selling handbook to help understand the stages of grief in many types of losses.

For Friends and Family

Helping Others to Cope with Grief

Bockelman, Wilfred. *Finding the Right Words*. Minneapolis: Augsburg Fortress, 1990.
Practical suggestions for offering care and comfort from a Christian spiritual perspective.

Grollman, Earl A. *Talking About Death, A Dialogue Between Parent and Child*. Boston: Beacon Press, 1970.
Sensitive, straightforward discussion of death designed to be read to children ages three to eight. Illustrated.

Jewett, Claudia. *Helping Children Cope with Separation & Loss*. Boston: The Harvard Common Press Inc., 1982.
A clear, practical discussion with examples of children losing parents through death or divorce.

Levine, Stephen. *Meetings at the Edge*. New York: Anchor Press/Doubleday, 1984.
Skillfully written and compassionate dialogues with the grieving and the dying.

Levine, Stephen. *Who Dies?* New York: Anchor Press/Doubleday, 1982.
Rooted in wisdom and compassion, this profound and readable work addresses many aspects of the dying process and grief.

Lord, Janice Harris. *Beyond Sympathy*. Ventura: Pathfinder Publishing, 1988.
Suggestions and examples of how to help those in grief.

Manning, Doug. *Comforting Those Who Grieve*. New York: Harper & Row, 1987.
Pastoral guide for friends and counselors to understand

how people feel while recovering from loss and how to help them.

Morgan, Ernest. *Dealing Creatively with Death.* North Carolina: Celo Press, 1988.
A resource book and manual on death education with extensive appendixes.

Murphey, Cecil. *Comforting Those Who Grieve.* Atlanta: John Knox Press, 1979.
A sensitive little book with specific suggestions.

Ram Dass and Paul Gorman. *How Can I Help?* New York: Knopf, 1987.
A book of rich insights into the human condition. Practical wisdom that comes from the heart.

For Children and Adolescents

Ages Three to Eight

Althea. *When Uncle Bob Died.* London: Dinosaur Publications, 1982.
Touches on many aspects of death of concern to children. Illustrated and accessible.

Cohen, Miriam. *Jim's Dog Muffins.* New York: Greenwillow Books, 1984.
Exquisite little book with colorful illustrations capturing the natural grief responses of a first-grader when his dog is run over and killed. Ages three to five.

Fassler, Joan. *My Grandpa Died Today.* New York: Human Sciences Press, 1971.
After his grandfather dies, young David struggles to understand and accept the death. In doing so, he comes to appreciate a little bit more about the joy of life. Ages three to five.

Greenberg, Judith, and Helen Carey. *Sunny: The Death of a Pet.* New York: Franklin Watts, 1986.

Simple narrative story of the death of a loved dog. Addresses healthy grief responses in young children.

Millonie, Bryan, and Robert Ingpen. *Lifetimes: The Beautiful Way to Explain Death to Children.* New York: Bantam, 1983. About beginnings and endings in plants, animals, and people. Lovely illustrations. Ages three to five.

St. Christopher's Hospice. *Someone Special Has Died.* London: St. Christopher's Hospice Department of Social Work, 1989.
Candidly treats key issues likely to be of concern to young children.

Ages Five to Ten

Cohn, Janice. *I Had a Friend Named Peter.* New York: William Morrow and Company, Inc., 1987.
Reassuring and sensitive story to help a child face the loss of a young friend. Excellent guideline chapter for parents and teachers.

Geller, Norman. *Talk to God . . . I'll Get the Message.* Lewiston, ME: Norman Geller, 1983.
Story of a loving relationship between a dying grandfather and his grandson as they face the grandfather's impending death. Excellent material for understanding and discussion. Format:Protestant/Catholic/Jewish versions.

Gould, Deborah. *Grandpa's Slide Show.* New York: Lothrop, Lee & Shepard Books, 1987.
Loving and candid story of a grandfather, his death, his family's grief, and his grandson's poignant and natural responses. Ages five to eight.

Harris, Audrey. *Why Did He Die?* Minneapolis: Lerner Publications Company, 1965.
A mother's explanation to her young son upon the death of his friend's grandfather. Straightforward in substance, metered in form. Ages five to eight.

Jukes, Mavis. *Blackberries in the Dark.* New York: Knopf, 1985.
Tender account of a grandmother and her grandson as

they grieve, reminisce, and eventually create new family traditions to replace those identified with the grandfather who has died.

Kübler-Ross, Elisabeth. *Remember the Secret.* Berkeley: Celestial Arts, 1982.
Christian message of hope in the face of loss as the reality of death is faced by two children.

Viorst, Judith. *The Tenth Good Thing About Barney.* New York: Atheneum, 1983.
Charmingly illustrated book about the death and burial of a pet cat. Ages five to eight.

Helping Children Prepare for the Death of Loved Ones

Brackett, Rona Novis. *Harry's Grandpa Takes a Mysterious Journey.* Sonoma, CA: Arcus Publishing Company, 1986.
A young Jewish boy learns to accept his grandfather's imminent death with the help of a loving family and dreams. Addresses issues such as the grandfather's increasingly poor appearance and dependency during hospitalization for cancer.

Miles, Miska. *Annie and the Old One.* Boston: Little, Brown and Company, 1971.
Poignant tale of a Navajo child's attempt to prevent her grandmother's death by interfering with the completion of the grandmother's "last" weaving. As the story ends, Annie recognizes that all things are a part of the earth.

Adolescents

Asher, Sandy. *Missing Pieces.* New York: Delacorte Press, 1984.
A teenager copes with her own and her mother's grief following the death of her father. A romance helps her accept her mother's grief.

Blume, Judy. *Tiger Eyes.* New York: Dell, 1981.
Davey's attempts to deal with grief after her father's death are complicated by her mother's sudden depression.

Cleaver, Vera. *Belle Pruitt.* New York: Lippincott, 1988.
Novel of an eleven-year-old's world when her baby brother dies.

Klein, Stanley. *The Final Mystery.* Garden City, NJ: Doubleday, 1974.
Fascinating academic exploration of the meaning of death and how people of different times and cultures have dealt with the issue.

LeShan, Eda. *Learning to Say Good-bye: When a Parent Dies.* New York: Avon Books, 1976.
An easy-to-understand, warm, and compassionate book to help adolescents move through grief and on to hope.

Paterson, Katherine. *Bridge to Terabithia.* New York: Thomas Y. Crowell Company, 1972.
A Newbery Award–winning tale of adolescent friendship and the anguish and coping of young Jess when his friend, Leslie, drowns.

Payne, Jr., Bernal C. *The Late, Great Dick Hart.* Boston: Houghton Mifflin, 1986.
Fantasy in which an adolescent boy dies but reappears to his grieving friend and invites him to join him in the perfect world that exists after death.

Richter, Elizabeth. *Losing Someone You Love: When a Brother or Sister Dies.* New York: Putnam's, 1986.
Fifteen young adults who have lost a brother or sister write about their feelings and difficulties at home and at school.

Stolz, Mary. *The Edge of Next Year.* New York: Harper & Row, 1974.
A fourteen-year-old boy copes with the death of his mother and the alienation that divides his grief-stricken family.

Helping Adolescents Prepare for the Death of Loved Ones

Holl, Kristi. *The Rose Beyond the Wall.* New York: Atheneum, 1985.

Novel about an adolescent girl's relationship with her dying grandmother. Sensitive and well written.

For Professionals and Those with Further Interest

Bowlby, John. *Attachment and Loss,* 2 vols. New York: Basic Books, 1969–1973.

Bowlby, John. *Attachment and Loss,* vol. 3. London: Hogarth Press, 1980

Bridges, William. *Transitions: Making Sense of Life's Changes.* New York: Addison-Wesley, 1980.

Cochran, Larry, and Emily Claspell. *The Meaning of Grief.* New York: Greenwood Press, 1987.

Grollman, Earl A. (ed.). *Explaining Death to Children.* Boston: Beacon Press, 1967.

Hartsough, D. M., and D. G. Meyers. *Disaster Work and Mental Health: Prevention and Control of Stress Among Workers.* Rockville, MD: National Institute of Mental Health, 1985.

Kübler-Ross, Elisabeth. *Death: The Final Stage of Growth.* Englewood Cliffs, NJ: Prentice-Hall, 1975.

Kübler-Ross, Elisabeth. *On Death and Dying.* New York: Macmillan, 1969.

Mills, G., R. Reisler, A. Robinson, and G. Vermilye. *Discussing Death: A Guide to Death Education.* Ann Arbor, MI: ETC Publications, 1976.

Osterweis, Marian, and Jessica Townsend. *Health Professionals and the Bereaved.* Rockville, MD: U.S. Department of Health and Human Services. DHHS Publication No. (ADM) 88-1552, 1988 (pamphlet).

Parkes, Colin Murray. *Bereavement.* London: Tavistock, 1972.

Parkes, Colin Murray, and Robert S. Weiss. *Recovery from Bereavement.* New York: Basic Books, 1983.

Philpot, Terry (ed.). *Last Things: Social Work with the Dying and the Bereaved.* Surrey, England: Reed Business Publishing, 1989.

Raphael, Beverly. *The Anatomy of Bereavement.* New York: Basic Books, 1983.

Sanders, Catherine. *Grief, the Mourning After.* New York: Wiley, 1989.

Schneidman, E. S. *Voices of Death.* New York: Harper & Row, 1980.

Worden, William J. *Grief Counseling and Grief Therapy: A Handbook for the Mental Health Practitioner.* New York: Springer, 1982.

Index

Grateful acknowledgment is made for permission to reprint:

Excerpt from *A Grief Observed* by C. S. Lewis is reprinted with the permission of HarperCollins Publishers. Copyright © 1961 by N. W. Clerk.

Excerpt from *On Death and Dying* by Elisabeth Kübler-Ross is reprinted with the permission of Macmillan Publishing Company. Copyright © 1969 by Elisabeth Kübler-Ross.

'Abdu'l-Bahá, *Selections from the Writings of 'Abdu'l-Bahá*, compiled by the Research Department of the Universal House of Justice, trans. Committee at the Bahá'í World Centre and Marzieh Gail (Haifa: Bahá'í World Centre, 1978), pp. 199–200, reprinted by permission.

Material adapted from *What Do You Do Now?* used with permission from the Life Insurance Marketing and Research Association, Inc.: Farmington, CT.

Excerpts from "Analysis of Sympathy Greeting Card Sentiments," by Steven R. Johnson, reprinted courtesy of American Greetings Corp.

Letter from *A Letter of Consolation* by Henri J. M. Nouwen. Copyright © 1982 by Henri J. M. Nouwen. Reprinted by permission of HarperCollins Publishers.

Excerpt from *The Letters of Edith Wharton*, edited by R. W. B. Lewis and Nancy Lewis. Copyright © 1988 by R. W. B. Lewis, Nancy Lewis, and William R. Tyler. Reprinted by permission of Charles Scribner's Sons, an imprint of Macmillan Publishing Company.

Excerpt from "God of the Open Air, VII" in *The Poems of Henry Van Dyke* (New York: Charles Scribner's Sons, 1911).

Excerpt from *How Can I Help?* by Ram Dass and Paul Gorman. Copyright © 1985 by Ram Dass and Paul Gorman. Reprinted by permission of Alfred A. Knopf, Inc.

Excerpt from *The Ultimate Loss* by Joan Bordow, reprinted by permission of Beaufort Books, Inc.

About the Authors

Leonard M. Zunin, M.D., senior psychiatric consultant for the California Department of Mental Health, has led a distinguished and unique career in psychiatry both in private practice and public service, and as a researcher and lecturer. For more than twenty years, Dr. Zunin has explored the phenomenon of greeting and parting, attachment and loss, and the special issues facing the bereaved and terminally ill. In 1968, while chief of psychiatry at Camp Pendleton, California, he initiated "Operation Second Life," a groundbreaking program for Vietnam widows. After the military, Dr. Zunin worked in private practice with terminally ill patients. This led him to a period of intense spiritual study and brought him to the Far East. For several years he lived and worked in Nepal and India as a consultant in psychiatry, and evaluated Eastern techniques for use in psychotherapy. He is the author of the bestselling book on communication, *Contact: The First Four Minutes,* was the director of the Institute for Reality Therapy, and has consulted for numerous organizations, including the U.S. State Department, the Center for Prisoner of War Studies, and the Peace Corps.

Hilary Stanton Zunin teaches English, creative writing, and Shakespeare at Napa High School. An expert on the effect of grief on school-aged children, she conducts workshops for teachers on "Learning Through Loss." She has traveled extensively throughout Europe, India, and Africa. She formerly worked as a parachuting instructor and held two world's records as a member of a women's skydiving team. Before her return to teaching, she was an account supervisor in public relations, specializing in food and wine clients in the United States and Europe. She and her husband, Leonard, live in Napa, California.